SPIRIT BY THE SEA TRILOGY

SEEING THE PLAN - BOOK THREE

APRIL AUTRY

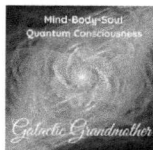

ALSO BY APRIL AUTRY

Galactic Grandmother Past Life Series

ATLANTIS, JOURNEY FROM THE INNER TEMPLE

MY LIFE WITH JESUS

ESCAPE FROM MALDEK

Galactic Grandmother Spiritual Journey Series

WORKING IN THE QUANTUM FIELD, BOOK 1 & 2

MULTIDIMENSIONAL ASPECTS - HIGHER SELVES

CHAPTER 1

As Konani had dreamed, I sat in the boat looking back at him and Laka waving to me. My brothers and their families, the holy man's brothers and their families, stood with the villagers and waved. They yelled to us, "Safe travels," and I felt sad. I was leaving my family, my island, and going into the sea that never ended. Milana said she could guide us to the island where Kekoa waited, and I prayed to the ancestors.

"Be with us. Protect us."

The boat went up and down on the smooth waters past the waves. I looked at the young warriors that sat between me and Milana. They were strong, and wanted to travel to the new village. Milana and I were also strong, and had fought in battle.

"Turn! Milana yelled, we pushed our paddles into the water on one side of the boat, and pulled back, to force the boat forward. We moved away from our friends and family, following the island as we had done before, yet now we would not stop at the end of the island. We would go into the water that met the sky, and travel under the sun, then under the moon.

. . .

THE BOAT WAS LONG, Milana sat in the front, and I sat in the back. The young warriors sat between us. We moved the boat quickly through the water, as Milana had taught us. She told us that we would not stop, until we reached the new village. We would sleep while others paddled, then paddle while they slept. We would drink water, eat dried fruit, fish, and keep moving.

"We will travel with the sea birds each day, and with the stars Kekoa showed me, at night." Milana told us.

We traveled past the end of our island, and I looked back. I saw the dark waves of deep water, rolling in and crashing on the rocks of the tall mountain. I looked up to see a thin line that cut across the mountain, and knew it was the high trail that I had walked from village to village. I took in a long breath, and tried to smell the land, as we pulled away.

"I enjoyed being a medicine man." I thought.

"You are a medicine man now." my teacher whispered.

I looked away from the island, and to the water ahead.

"Yes," I thought, "the ancestors picked me, the holy man trained me, and I will make medicine on any island."

Then I wondered what plants I would find on the new island, and my thoughts took me away from leaving.

"KAI!" Milana yelled, "Kai!"

I looked up to see Milana pointing ahead.

"What is it?" I yelled back.

"The big boat."

I looked hard, yet only saw a small boat where the water met the sky.

"Where has it been?" I said, "has it attacked the new village?"

"Kekoa will protect the new village." Milana called back.

"Yes!" shouted one of the young warriors.

"Kekoa will win the battle!" another cried.

I thought of the big boat with many men. These men did not have good hearts, they took young women from their families, and carried sickness. A sickness that killed our grandfathers and grandmothers, just as their long blade had killed the holy man. These men made us fight to protect our island, and I wondered if they returned, could we still protect it?

"Will we always fight?" I thought, "will I never have peace again?"

WE PUSHED HARDER to travel fast. The sun was hot, making water pour down from our faces and bodies. We took small drinks from our water pouches, and ate the dried fruit and fish as we traveled. We watched the sea birds fly over our heads, and went with them toward the island that we could not yet see. The sea water swelled up and down, and we pushed the boat through it, without stopping. The day felt long, and when the sun sank into the sea, the cool wind that blew felt good.

"Can you sleep?" Milana asked a young man.

"Yes!" he shouted.

The others laughed, I knew we all wanted to stop paddling, and close our eyes.

"I will sleep." another said.

"Good." Milana said, "lay down in the boat." and she pointed to where each would sleep.

Milana looked at me, and I nodded.

"She guides us well." I thought.

The sky darkened, and the bright lights came out. Milana pointed to the lights,

"We travel there." she said.

I looked at the lights in the sky, then down, and did not see where the night sky ended or the dark water began. We traveled through darkness, above us and below. I felt peace come into me, and my heart opened to the feeling of being part of this place, where Father God and Mother Earth joined. Water came into my eyes, I breathed in, and felt great happiness. We paddled on, not speaking, and listened to the sounds of the water, paddles and boat. My thoughts rested, and I looked ahead to the sea going up and down.

. . .

"KAI!" Milana called.

I saw a young man getting up from his sleep.

"You sleep." she said.

"Yes." I called back, ready to rest.

She pointed for me to sleep at my end of the boat. I slid my paddle down into the the boat, and started to stand.

"Oh!" I said out loud, when my legs were too stiff to move. I put my hands down on each side of me, and pushed myself up. I bent my legs, moved back and forth with the boat, then kicked each leg to make them move. I climbed down in front of my seat, and lay down on my side. My arms hurt from using them, yet after closing my eyes, I soon felt nothing.

I AWOKE to the boat slamming down into the water. I sat up, and wind blew into my face. I saw Milana, sitting at the front of the boat, as it started to go up a tall wave.

"Paddle!" she screamed over the noise of the wind and water.

I jumped up on my seat, and grabbed the paddle. I quickly dug it into the water, with the others. I saw dark clouds blowing toward us on the wind, and the lights in the sky were hidden by them. The boat raised up on the water where Milana sat, and she leaned forward as if to hold it down.

"Paddle!" she screamed again.

The wind blew against us, waves pulled and pushed at the boat, yet we paddled hard to move the boat through the water. I looked at the warriors in front of me. Their arms and backs were strong, they dug the paddles in, and pulled them back. I was glad Milana had picked these young men to go with us.

We fought the water and wind, moving slowly under the dark clouds. Then water began to pour down on our heads, and into my eyes. I could only see the men in front of me, and I wondered how we would find our way to the island.

"Paddle!" Milana yelled again.

The boat was hit hard by a wave, and threw Milana back from her seat, into the men behind her. I thanked the ancestors for protecting her, and not letting her fall out of the boat.

Men were getting sick, the dried fish and fruit would not stay in their bellies, yet they held strong to their paddles. The water that blew with the wind was cold, my body began to shake, and my arms and shoulders burned as I used them.

"Keep us strong." I asked the ancestors.

We were tired, I saw the men strain as they pulled the paddles through the water, and the boat moved slower. Finally, the wind pushed the clouds past, the water stopped coming down, and lights in the sky came out again. The big waves left also, and the boat was easier to move through the water.

"Thank you." I thought.

"Drink water!" I yelled, knowing this would help the men.

The men begin to do this, and I did also. Suddenly my belly turned, and my mouth filled with the fish I had swallowed. I quickly leaned over the side, and the fish flew into the water. I wiped my mouth, then washed my hand in the sea. My head felt sick also. I took in a breath, and looked past the men to Milana. She still paddled, and I wondered if she had slept, or felt sick.

THE NIGHT PASSED SLOWLY, before the sun started to light the sky. Milana stood up, and turned around.

"I will sleep," she said, then pointed to a man, "you will also."

The young man was happy to climb down into the boat, and rest. Milana looked back at me, climbed down into the boat, and turned on her side.

The men and I pushed our tired, sick bodies to work, and did not talk as we paddled. I watched the sun come up, then we saw large fish swimming with us. They jumped up out of the water, then dove back in.

"They swim fast!" a young man said.

"Look!' another yelled, and pointed across the water.

I looked to see where he pointed, and far away above the water, saw the top of an island.

The men called out, and I also felt happy.

Milana sat up, "What is this?"

A young man pointed to the island, Milana stood up, and looked at the island. She untied the string holding her long hair, and shook it loose. I watched her straight hair blow, and fall to her legs. She gathered it in her hands, tied it again, and moved from one leg to the another. Her body was strong, and I liked to watch her move. I looked at the others in the boat, and they also watched Milana. She could pick any man to join with her, yet she did not. She was a warrior, a medicine woman, and she did not want the life of other women.

Milana pointed to the island, "The sun will go down, rise, and go down again. We will arrive at the new village in darkness of night."

The men called out, happy to know this.

"Good!" I yelled up to her.

She smiled, and lay back down in the boat to sleep.

This day passed slowly, we could see the island, yet it was still far away. We were tired and sore, yet happy no clouds could be seen. After Milana awoke, she spoke of the new village.

"I have built a hut, and you will also." she told us.

"When will we return to our families?" a young man asked.

"Kekoa will tell you." she said.

"Look!" another yelled, and pointed to more of the large fish swimming fast, jumping out of the water, then diving back down, many fish passed, and we enjoyed watching them.

"I have seen these fish swim in the waves!" I yelled.

I took a drink from my pouch, and a bite of dried fruit. Now my hungry belly kept the food, and I ate more. The sun was low to the water, and when darkness came, we were happy that we would see the new village soon. We paddled through the night, with some sleeping, and I again felt peace fill me.

When Milana told me to sleep, I lay down on the wet wood, and closed my eyes. Suddenly I saw the holy man. He smiled at me, then was gone. I opened my eyes, and knew that I was not yet asleep, the holy man had not been in a dream.

"He smiled." I thought, and knew he traveled with us.

"Thank you." I whispered to him, then closed my eyes.

I AWOKE to the sun on my body. I pushed myself up to sit, and my body hurt from not moving. I used my hands to stand up, and bent my legs to move with the boat. I picked up each foot and wiggled it, then moved my arms around, to help my stiff bones.

"I will be happy to walk again!" I said to the others.

The men laughed. "We will be glad also!"

Milana turned to look at us, "When you step on the sand, your body will still move like the water, and you will fall."

"I will be happy to fall on land!" a young man called out, and we laughed with him.

7

CHAPTER 2

The sun rose above us, and I could see the island more clearly. It rose high from the water with tall mountains, and clouds hid the high peaks. I thought of the mountains I traveled, from village to village, giving medicine.

"It looks like our island!" I yelled.

This made me happy, and I started to sing. The others joined me, and we sang songs from our villages. We paddled, looking toward the island, and I thought of what I would see there. I wondered if Kekoa had fought the men on the big boat. The boat we saw could be leaving after battle, or it could be traveling around the island, looking for a safe place to land.

"I will be glad to see Kekoa, and learn if there was a battle." I yelled to Milana.

She turned to me, "If Kekoa fought them, they will not return!"

The men yelled out, and laughed, "They will not return!"

"I will show you the new island." she called back.

"I want to see the plants we can use for medicine."

She nodded.

"I will enjoy making medicine again!" I told her.

. . .

THE LOWER THE sun got to the water, and the closer we got to the island, the more I wanted to get out of the boat. I would be happy to fall on the sand, as Milana told us, to stop paddling and get out of the boat. I sang more, so I would not think of this, and watched the island grow larger. When darkness began to fall around us, and the first lights came into the sky, I yelled out.

"We thank the ancestors for protecting us, and bringing us to the island."

"Yes!" The men shouted.

"We thank Milana for guiding us." I called out.

"I thank Kekoa for teaching me." she yelled.

"We will paddle behind the waves, then travel along the island, until we find a fire pit." Milana told us.

We paddled, and soon heard the crashing waves.

"Turn!" Milana yelled, and pointed.

We dug the paddles into the water, and turned the boat. We started traveling along the island, and looked ahead for a fire pit. We traveled to the end of the island, then around the mountain that came down into the water. As we came around the rocks and mountain, we saw the light of a fire.

"There!" Milana yelled.

The others yelled, and I did also.

We paddled quickly, and saw villagers standing around the fire pit.

"Stop!" Milana told us. "Turn toward the sand."

We did as she said, then sat there, in the darkness of the water facing the fire pit.

"Kekoa!" Milana yelled loudly.

Then the men yelled, "Kekoa!" "Kekoa!"

The villagers turned, and looked at the water.

"Kekoa!" Milana yelled again.

The villagers walked to the water.

"Kekoa!" she yelled again.

"Milana!" A low voice yelled back.

We all yelled, and laughed. We had arrived!

"Thank you!" I said to my teacher.

"We will ride the waves!" Milana told us.

WE PADDLED WITH THE WAVES. We rose to the top, then dropped down, with the water pushing the boat forward. Then another wave came behind us, and pushed us closer to the sand. We paddled until we heard the sand under the boat. Milana jumped out of the boat, and hung on, as she started to fall. Then the men jumped out, each grabbing the boat to stand. I jumped out, held on to the boat, and we pulled it from the water to dry sand.

"Welcome!" Kekoa yelled loudly.

We stepped away from the boat, and started to fall down. I watched Milana grab a young man, so she would not fall, yet he also fell to the sand. Kekoa laughed, and reached down to pull Milana to her feet. As she told us, I fell down on the sand when I tried to walk.

"Kai!" I heard Kekoa yell as he lifted me up.

I saw villagers, and Kekoa's warriors, helping the men.

"Kekoa!" I said, grabbing his arm, "it is good to see you!"

My legs were stiff, and did not want to walk. We walked slowly to the fire pit, and were given food and water.

"We have much to tell you." Milana told Kekoa.

"You must eat and rest this night", he told her, "we will speak when the sun rises."

We sat around the fire and ate. The hot fish tasted good, and the water they gave me, had a new taste I liked.

"Now," Kekoa said, "our travelers will drink this, and sleep."

He gave Milana a pouch that she sipped from.

"I know this!" she said, and took a big, long drink from the pouch, before passing it to me.

I leaned my head back, and drank from the pouch. The fruit juice burned my throat as it went down, and warmed my belly.

"Good?" Kekoa asked, and smiled.

"Good!" I answered, and took another drink, before passing it away.

We drank more of the fruit juice, and my eyes grew tired.

Kekoa clapped me on the back, "Come! I will take you and Milana to my hut, and the others will sleep with my warriors."

I followed Kekoa and Milana down the path, to his hut, and lay down on a mat. My head still moved with the sea, yet I fell into a deep sleep.

I AWOKE to the sounds of a village. I heard children, men and women. I smelled fish being cooked, and my belly told me to eat. I turned to my side, and pushed with my hands to sit up.

"Ohhh!" My shoulders and arms hurt. Then I stood, and my legs felt like logs, stiff and sore.

"I need medicine!" I thought to myself.

I looked around, and saw that Kekoa and Milana were gone. I walked to the doorway, and looked out. The sun shone brightly on many huts and villagers. They were caring for children, preparing fish and fruit, weaving baskets, talking and laughing. I walked down the path, saw villagers that I knew from the old island, and they waved and smiled. These people had not been through a battle. They were not thinking of fighting, hiding, or of the sickness that made the elders pass.

Milana and Kekoa sat eating at the fire pit, and I walked to them.

"Welcome." Kekoa said, "Eat!" he told me, and pointed to the hot fish laying on a palm leaf. I grabbed one, and enjoyed the new taste.

"What kind of fish is this?" I asked.

"This is from the water here." he said, and pointed to the sea.

"I like it." I ate the fish, then grabbed a piece of fruit.

"I told Kekoa about our battle." Milana said.

I nodded, and took another bite of fruit.

"They did not come here." Kekoa told me.

"I swallowed my fruit, and wiped my mouth, "I know this."

Kekoa looked at me, and I told him, "The villagers are happy here."

Kekoa nodded, "There is a village on the other side."

"We have to know if they are on the island." I said.

Kekoa nodded, "I will take warriors to the other village, and leave others here."

"We travel!" Milana said, and stood up.

Kekoa looked at her, and patted the log where she had been sitting.

"Sit" he said, and watched her sit down again.

"Milana has told me of the battle," he said, "yet I will know of Aukamu's passing."

He looked at me, and I nodded.

"The ancestors had prepared him, he knew of the men that came," I said, "after they took him, he guided us."

Kekoa shook his head, and looked down.

"We prepared the villagers before the battle, then again before we left."

"Tell me of this." Kekoa said.

I TOLD him of making piles of spears around small fire pits, of building huts in the mountains for the women and children to hide, and how we left them with trained young men to watch all sides of the island.

"This is good." he said, and looked at Milana, "you have trained young men there, and you will train here also."

"The villagers on this island need to be prepared." I told him.

Milana nodded.

"Kai," Kekoa said, "ask the ancestors to protect us, and ask the holy man to guide us."

I nodded, "He is with us."

"I will send warriors into the mountains, to build huts for our villagers." Kekoa said.

"I will take them around the island, and make camps to watch for the boat." Milana told us.

"It is good you built the village here." I said, "It is protected by the mountain behind, and on the sides, where the mountains go down to the water.

"There is a path going into the mountains that the villagers could use, then close with rocks, to keep others out." Kekoa told me.

"Good." I nodded.

Kekoa and Milana spoke of training warriors, and I thought of preparing the villagers. I also thought of making medicine, and traveling to the other village.

"Will we have no peace?" I asked my teacher.

"Kai!" I heard Milana say, and I turned to look at her.

Kekoa and Milana laughed

"You were thinking?" Kekoa asked.

"Thinking of peace, and wanting to be a medicine man again."

Kekoa clapped me on the back, and looked into my eyes, "There will be peace again."

I looked at him, "I want this.

"Milana, I will take Kai to the other village," Kekoa said, "you will stay, and start training warriors."

Milana made a face, started to speak, then stopped and nodded her head.

I smiled at her, "We will travel this island soon."

"We leave when the sun rises." Kekoa said, and stood.

I finished eating, and watched children play by the water. The village men gathered wood, and put it by the fire pit. I enjoyed seeing this village, and thought of the village I grew in with my family.

"Thank you for these blessings." I felt good to be sitting here, and not in the boat on the water.

"Tea?" an old woman asked me,

I smiled, and nodded. I had not drank hot tea since leaving the old island, and knew I would enjoy sipping it now.

"I do not want to travel in a boat again." I thought, yet I knew that I must, to see my brothers and Konani.

I watched Milana gather young men, to be trained as warriors. She took them to the sand by the water.

"If you fall on your back in a battle," she said, and lay down on her back in the sand, "you can still fight."

"Come here," she pointed to a young man, "stand over my legs."

The young man spread his legs to stand over her, and looked at the others with a big smile. Milana quickly dug her feet into the sand, pushed herself out from under his legs, while lifting her hips and kicking at his legs, then jumped to her feet. The young man fell back.

"Are you hurt?" she asked, and helped him up.

He shook his head, while the others laughed.

"Do this, yet do not kick hard." she told them, "In battle, you will kick hard."

She watched as they fought on the sand, and she showed them how to move in a fight.

"She is a good teacher." I thought.

I wanted to swim, and stretched my arms up.

"Ohh." My shoulders and back hurt.

"I will rest." I thought, and wondered if Milana hurt. I watched her, then saw a little girl looking at me. I smiled at her, her eyes got big, and she ran away.

"She is afraid of me." I thought, and looked down at my body.

My skin was dark, and many wounds had made marks on my body. I was big, strong, and looked as a warrior.

I got up, and walked to a hut, where an old man sat weaving.

"Are you well?" I asked.

He smiled, with many teeth gone, "Yes."

"I am a medicine man, do you know a villager I can help?"

"My brother." he pointed across the path to another hut.

I walked to it, and looked in.

"Welcome."

A man sat on a mat, with his legs stretched out in front of him.

"Do you need medicine?" I asked.

He waved for me to come in, and pointed at his leg. It was swollen and looked hot. I reached down, and touched the skin.

"How long?"

"Many suns." he said.

I looked carefully at his leg, and found a small wound. I pointed to it, and he nodded.

"It was a bite." he told me, "I put mud on it."

I nodded, mud heals bites, yet this needed more.

"I will bring you medicine." I said, and walked out of his hut. I stood and looked around,

"What can I use?" I thought.

A young woman walked to me, and smiled.

"Welcome." she said.

I looked at her, she was pretty. "I need to make medicine." I told her.

"Can I help?" she asked.

I looked in her eyes, and knew she wanted to find a man to join with.

"No." I told her.

She smiled again. "I am glad to help."

I put my hand on her arm, "I have traveled with young warriors, that need new huts. Can you help them?"

Her eyes lit up, "I will weave mats for them!"

"Tell them Kai sent you to help."

She nodded and smiled, "Thank you." and walked toward the warriors' hut.

I watched her walk away, then followed her down the path. I saw her go to the young men, that came with me in the boat, and I smiled to myself.

"I wonder who will join with her!"

I walked past them to the water, where the waves crashed, and looked.

"I want the small plant that grows on the rocks, under the water." I thought, and walked into the water, waited for a wave to pull away, then used my blade to cut the soft, wet plant from the rock.

"Thank you." I spoke to the plant. I gathered a hand full, and put a small piece in my mouth. It tasted of the sea.

"This is good." I started back to the old man.

After cleaning his wound, I patted the plant on it, and wrapped it with a strip of cloth.

"The sea water, and this plant will draw out the poison." I told him.

"Good." he said.

15

"When the sun rises again, clean it, and put more on." I gave him the sea plant.

"If it does not heal, go sit with your leg in the sea water." I told him.

"I will."

I WALKED TO OTHER HUTS, and talked to many villagers. On our home island, the holy man had taught these villagers to make medicines, while he traveled. They did this, and helped each other.

"These are for sore bones." a grandmother showed me tea leaves.

"Yes." I said, "I have used these."

Many young women smiled as I passed, and I knew they would be happy to join with me, yet they felt as sisters. I walked to the mountain behind the village, and looked for the trail that Kekoa spoke of. I saw a break in the trees, walked there, and looked up.

"There."

The mountain rose high on each side of the trail, and the trail went behind large rocks. I knew these were the rocks, that would be used to close the trail. I looked around, and listened to the birds. This island looked as my old island, and I was glad I would travel with Kekoa to see it. My stomach made noise, and I thought of the good fish I ate.

"I want more!" I turned to walk back to the fire pit.

"You have eaten much!" Kekoa laughed.

I laughed, and looked at the bones on my palm leaf. We sat by the fire pit, and Milana told us of her new warriors.

"They thought I was a weak woman!" she said.

Kekoa and I laughed.

"I threw them on the sand," she said, and motioned with her arm, "then they listened."

Kekoa leaned his head back, and laughed loudly. He slapped his leg and shouted, "They will learn!"

THERE WERE dark clouds far out over the water, and as the sun went behind them, the clouds looked the colors of fruit and flowers. The flames in the fire pit grew high, and shown brightly. Heat from the fire warmed me, and as I watched the flames, the villagers gathered around. Some stood, while others sat on logs, and on the sand. The children now joined us, and sat quietly. I saw them, and thought of myself, watching the holy man call for the ancestors.

I stood up, closed my eyes, and raised my arms in the air. I thought of the holy man, my father and mother, and the villagers that passed from sickness. My heart hurt, I wanted to see them again, and to speak with them.

"Ancestors be with us!" I yelled with a deep voice, "Protect us and guide us!"

I opened my eyes, looked at the villagers, then back to the fire. I dropped my arms, closed my eyes and took in a big breath, before slowly blowing the air out. When I opened my eyes, I saw them. The ancestors stood around, among the villagers. I felt the holy man, and knew he was also with us.

"Thank you for being here." I cried out.

The villagers yelled out, "Thank you!" and clapped their hands. Many villagers also felt the ancestors, and began to speak to them.

I looked at Kekoa, and he yelled, "Akamu guide us!"

Milana stood quietly, her eyes filled with water, I knew that she thought of her grandfather. I saw him beside her, yet she did not.

The villagers were happy, and grandmothers began to sing a song that I knew from the old village. I smiled, and started to sing with them. Then an ancestor came to me, and asked me to speak to his family. I looked at him, and saw a long mark from a wound, on his face.

"Tell her she will have a girl." he pointed to a young woman, whose belly stood out with child. "Tell her I will watch over the baby."

I walked to the woman, and told her.

"Who was this man?" she asked.

"I do not know," I said, "he had a long mark here." and I pointed to my face.

She smiled, "Uncle!"

The grandmother standing next to her smiled, and clapped her hands. "My brother will watch over her." and they began to speak of the uncle, and brother, that had passed many moons ago.

THE FIRE WAS LOW, and the villagers now tired, went into their huts. Kekoa and Milana had also gone to the hut to sleep. I wanted to sleep, yet many thoughts came to me. I walked to the sand that looked over the water, and sat down. Air blew over me, and I listened to the waves roll in. I pushed my feet into the warm sand, and dug my hands into it. Many lights sparkled in the night sky, and I felt my body start to rest. I lay back on the sand, with my hands behind my head, and looked up.

"This is the peace I want."

"You take this peace with you." my teacher whispered.

I closed my eyes, and fell into the peace of sleep.

I AWOKE to poking in my arm. I lay on my side, and felt it again. A small finger poked my arm, I rolled on to my back, and looked up through tired eyes. The little girl I had scared away, stood looking down at me.

"What is your name?" I asked her.

"Calea."

I sat up, "My name is Kai."

She smiled a little, and leaned her head to the side, "You have sand on your face."

I touched my face, and sand covered it where I slept.

"I will swim, and wash it off." I told her, and jumped to my feet.

I ran to the water, and stood with my feet in. Calea ran up beside me, then ran further into the water.

"Do not follow me!" I told her, as I ran past into the deeper water.

I dove under a wave, and came up on the other side. The water was warm, and I liked stretching my arms and legs to swim. I swam to the top of a wave coming in, and rolled over on my back, to float after it had passed.

"I need to swim more!" I thought.

I went up and down, on top of the water, then heard my name called,

"Kai!"

I raised my head, saw Milana waving to me, and I waved back. She waved for me to come in, so I swam to catch a wave, and rode it. When I reached shallow water, I stood and walked to her. I looked for the small girl, yet she was gone. Milana stood watching me, and when I reached her, she looked at my feet, my body, then my face.

"You are a strong man." she said.

I laughed, and felt my face get hot.

"Kekoa wants you to eat before you leave." she told me, and turned to walk away.

I watched her, and liked her body as she moved.

"You are a strong woman!"

She shook her head, laughed, and kept walking.

KEKOA WATCHED ME EAT. "We will travel on the mountain trail." he said.

I chewed my food, and nodded.

"We will sleep on the mountain this night, and travel far on the other side of the island, to reach the village."

"Is the village old?" I asked.

Kekoa shook his head, "The villagers came from the island where I was a boy."

"After the battle that you fought?"

"Yes, villagers came here, and to our old island."

"Tell me of this." I said.

"My family was strong, we fished in deep water for the big fish, yet we were not warriors. When our village was attacked, my father and brothers were returning from fishing. I fought to save my family. I tried to protect my mother and sisters, yet I could not, and saw them pass. I was cut many times by their blades, and when I lay on the ground ready to join my mother, my father and brothers reached us. My father carried me to a boat, and laid me in it, to leave with the others. I was told that my father and brothers fought to protect our boat as we left, before they fell and passed."

"Your father is glad that you lived." I told him, "he fought so you could live."

Kekoa nodded, and I saw water in his eyes, before he looked down.

I finished my food, "I am ready."

CHAPTER 3

I carried a small basket, and a bed roll that Kekoa gave me. I also carried my water pouch, and blade on my waist. My arms and legs felt good this day, I was ready to travel with Kekoa, to see the new island. I wanted to see the village on the other side, and learn the plants that grow here. Kekoa led me out of the village, and we were followed by warriors. Other warriors shouted, and waved as we left. I knew Milana wanted to travel with us, and I looked back at her. She stood watching us, and I waved. I hoped that we were not walking toward another battle, yet being with Kekoa, made me feel safe.

Kekoa reached the small trail into the mountain, and turned to look at me.

"It is small." he told me.

He took off his basket and bedroll, held them above his head, then turned his body to slide between the mountain and the big rocks. I did the same, and after a few steps, the rocks stopped. We put on our bedrolls and baskets, then walked ahead. The trail was steep, and we were careful not to slide down the side. The trail led us deep into a narrow canyon, where the trees and plants grew thick. Kekoa stopped, put his pack down, then pulled a long blade out. My mouth fell open, a blade such as this, was used to kill the holy man.

"The men on the big boat carried these blades." I told him.

Kekoa looked at me, "A warrior found this washed up on the sand, with sea plants wrapped around it."

"It was dropped from the boat we saw." I said.

"The blade is sharp, it was not in the water long." he told me.

I took in a big breath, and shook my head.

"We go." he said, and swung the blade to cut plants away from the trail.

I watched Kekoa swing the blade, with great force at the plants.

"How can we fight such blades?" I thought.

I walked slowly behind Kekoa, as he cleared the trail.

"These plants grow fast over the trail." he told me.

Water rolled down his big body as he worked, and I looked at the many battle marks, on his arms and back.

"You are the strongest man I know." I told him.

Kekoa laughed, "I am an old man!"

I laughed, "An old man that could crush me!"

The warriors behind me also laughed.

Kekoa worked until he tired, then stopped, and reached for his water pouch.

I grabbed mine, and took a drink. "Where will we sleep this night?"

"We will come to water, follow it up to a waterfall, where we can swim and sleep."

I nodded, "Good."

As Kekoa had told me, we came to a small stream, that passed over the trail.

"We go up!" he said.

Many trees grew out of the side of the mountain. Kekoa led us up beside a stream, and we climbed higher. Kekoa pulled himself up, to stand on a flat rock,

"There!" He pointed where I could not see.

I grabbed the rock where he stood, pulled myself up, to see we had reached flat land.

I saw a waterfall, and small pool of water below it.

"This is good!" I told him.

The water was not deep, yet I could wash my body. I filled my water pouch from the waterfall, and sat down next to Kekoa. We watched the warriors splash each other, laugh, and wrestle in the water.

"They will sleep well!" Kekoa said.

"I will also." I told him.

The warriors got out of the water, and sat in the sun to dry.

"Is this where the women and children will hide?" I asked, thinking it would be hard for them, to climb up the mountain.

"We will make steps, and tie ropes between the trees, they can hold the ropes as they climb." he said.

I nodded.

"The warriors will be close the trail with rocks, and stop men from following."

"This is a good plan."

Kekoa nodded, "I will send men to work on this, after I know the boat is not on the island."

"The villagers need to come here, and know where they will hide." I said.

"My village will be prepared," Kekoa said, "and we will also help the other village to prepare."

When the sun went behind the mountain, the light left quickly. The men made a fire, we ate, then lay down on our bed rolls. I was tired, and the men were also. Soon I heard sounds of them breathing loudly as they slept. I closed my eyes, and slept also.

I AWOKE to hearing my name.

"Kai!" I heard it again.

I sat up, and looked into the darkness where Kekoa and the men slept. I looked toward the waterfall, then into the trees behind me.

"Kai." he said, as I saw him.

Standing next to a tree was the holy man. I held my breath, and said nothing.

He smiled at me, and then slowly went away. My eyes filled with water.

"He is with us." I knew he was gone, yet I kept looking for him.

"Why was he here? Will he come back?" I sat thinking, until light started to come through the trees.

Kekoa made a noise, I looked at him, as he slowly sat up.

"My bones are getting old!" he laughed, and he stretched his legs out on the bed roll.

"The holy man was here." I told him. "he smiled."

"This is good," Kekoa said, "he did not warn us of battle."

"Yes," I said, "he was at peace."

I was glad the holy man came to me, yet I wondered why. I had a feeling that I would know soon.

We climbed back down the mountain, then walked along the trail. Kekoa walked fast, my long legs kept me behind him, yet I heard warriors breathing hard to stay with us. I heard a sea bird cry, and started to feel the cool air that blows from the water. The trail was leading us down, I saw the trees stopped growing, and the water beyond. Kekoa stopped, I walked up beside him, and he held his arm out to stop me. We stood on the side of the mountain, looking down, where the waves crashed against rocks below us.

"They cannot attack from this side." he said.

"You are well protected."

Then Kekoa stepped back, and walked into the trees, where I saw another trail along the top of the cliff.

We walked, watching where we put our feet, then we came to where dirt and rocks fell across the trail. Kekoa led us up, and we climbed over rocks, to the trail on the other side.

"Is there another trail to the village?" I asked.

"There is a trail that goes around the island, along the water."

"That trail is longer?"

"Yes, and I do not want to be seen." he told me.

24

We walked along the cliff until the sun went behind the water, then ate and slept beside the trail. When the sun rose, we started toward the village, and I wondered what we would do if the big boat was there.

I did not want to fight, and I did not want the men bringing sickness to this island. The trail led us away from the cliff, into the trees, where many plants grew. As I walked, I looked for plants that I could use for medicine.

"Oh!" I said out loud, when I saw the mountain tea bush. I walked off the trail, and started to pick leaves.

"Tea?" Kekoa asked.

"It is good for sore bones." I told him.

"I need this tea!" Kekoa shouted, and waited for me.

I picked many leaves, put them in my basket, and we started down the trail again.

"When the sun is close to the water," Kekoa said, "we will see the village."

The sun dropped down to the water, and I looked ahead to see the village. I also looked across the sea, and was glad I did not see the big boat.

"There!" shouted Kekoa, and pointed.

I saw palm trees that grew down to the sand. I did not see any huts, yet knew they must be in the shade of the trees.

"I do not see the boat." I told Kekoa.

"I wonder if the boat saw our villages." he said.

We left the trail, and walked down the cliff to the sand. When I reached the sand, I took off my sandals, and was glad to feel it under my feet. I ran to the water, and washed my feet. The men also took off their sandals, and joined me in the water.

Kekoa shook his head, "Warriors!" he shouted, and they ran back to him.

"You are not ready for battle," he told them, "when you carry sandals in your hands!"

I walked back to him, "They followed me."

He nodded, "They must follow me!" He looked at his men, "am I playing in the water?"

Kekoa turned, and walked down the beach. I looked at his men, as they quickly put their sandals on, and ran after him. I had not seen Kekoa angry with his men before.

"I am glad to be a medicine man." I thought.

As we walked under palm trees, I saw a hut, then many more. Soon I smelled fish cooking, and looked for the fire pit. A great fire burned in the fire pit, and villagers were gathered to eat. When the children saw us, they ran to us shouting, "Kekoa! Kekoa!"

I watched as this great warrior was greeted by the children, then the villagers, as we got closer to the fire pit.

"Welcome!" a man shouted, walking to Kekoa, and clapped him on the arm.

The men and I followed, and stood by Kekoa around the fire.

"This is Kai." Kekoa said, and pointed to me, "He is a medicine man from the old island."

"Welcome!" the villagers called to me.

"Kai told us of a big boat that attacked his village, and brought sickness."

The village men walked closer to me, "Speak of this."

I told them of the men on the big boat, how they killed the holy man, and many grandfathers and grandmothers with their sickness.

"This is bad!" they shouted.

"This boat did not pass our village, yet a man saw it from the mountain, as it went past the end of the island."

"I am glad it did not stop." I told them.

"You must be prepared." Kekoa told them, "if this boat returns."

"How do we prepare?" an elder asked.

Kekoa told them of training their young men to be warriors, of watching for the boat, and hiding their women and children.

"Will you train our men?" the villagers asked Kekoa.

I ate, then walked away from the fire pit, as Kekoa spoke to them.

"Thank you ancestors," I thought, "for protecting the villagers."

I walked to the sand, and looked at the water. I heard Kekoa talking and laughing with the village men, then speaking of the strong fruit juice they passed around.

The sky was dark, and women called for their children to come into their huts. These villagers were safe and happy, I was glad the children could sleep, and not think of bad men. I was also ready to sleep, and lay my bed roll down on the sand, where I could hear the waves. I lay back with my arms behind my head, and looked up at the lights, shining in the sky. I closed my eyes, and heard the holy man whisper.

"This is your new home."

I AWOKE to find the warriors, and Kekoa, sleeping on the sand around me. The sky had many clouds, which covered the sun, and kept the air cool. I quietly rolled up my blanket, and grabbed tea leaves from my basket. I walked to the fire pit, and asked a woman to use her pot for tea.

"Yes." she said, then poured water into it, from her large pouch.

"You are the medicine man?"

I put tea leaves in the water, and looked up at her, "Yes."

"My mother needs medicine."

"Is she sick?"

"When she walks, she hurts."

I nodded, thinking of the plants I would give her, "I will see her after my tea."

"Thank you." she said, and handed me a large fruit.

It was soft, I used my blade to cut away the outside, and inside the fruit was sweet and juicy.

"Thank you." I told her, enjoying the fruit.

"Have you made my tea?" I heard Kekoa's loud voice behind me.

"Yes!" I called back.

"Good!" he said, and walked to sit by me.

We sipped our tea, and spoke of what we would do.

"I will help the villagers prepare." Kekoa told me.

"I must give a woman medicine." I told him, "and look for plants that I can use."

"Good," he said, "we will stay here."

I looked at him, and wondered how long we would stay in this village.

"Milana prepares our village," Kekoa said, "we will prepare this village."

I enjoyed the cool air, and the clouds that hung in the sky. I watched village men leave in their fishing boats, and the women busy with their children. When the warriors joined Kekoa to eat, I left the fire pit, and went to find the woman that needed medicine. I walked down a trail that led between huts.

"Medicine man!"

I looked to see the woman that gave me fruit, standing by an old woman, and walked to them.

"Do you need medicine?" I asked the old woman.

"Yes," she said, "My legs are hard to walk."

"Let me see."

She began to walk slowly, without bending her legs. With each step she put out a stiff leg, leaning that way, then to the other side, as she went.

"Can I feel your leg?"

She nodded, I touched her leg where the bones came together, and felt many hard bumps where the leg should bend.

"The bones have grown together." she told me.

"I will give you leaves to make tea, then put the hot leaves on your legs."

"Thank you." she said.

I looked in her eyes, "Your legs will not heal, yet they will feel better."

She smiled, "When my mother was old, her legs grew like this."

I was glad she knew this. I reached in my basket, and gave her the mountain tea leaves.

"Thank you." the women said, as I walked away.

I looked up the trail going to the mountain, and wanted to see what plants grew there. I passed by many huts, the villagers smiled, and waved. I was happy that they had peace.

"Keep the boat away." I said to the ancestors.

THE TRAIL TOOK me out of the village, through fruit trees, then to a stream. I followed the stream, and watched the clear water, that ran over smooth rocks.

"Who are you?"

I stopped, and looked away from the water. A small girl stood on the trail ahead of me.

"I do not know you."

I smiled, "My name is Kai, I came here from another island."

"My name is Sael."

"Do you live in the village?" I asked.

She shook her head, "No, we live up there." and she pointed to the mountain.

"Take me to your hut." I said.

Sael turned, and I followed her up the trail.

We passed many bushes with flowers, and Sael stopped, to pick the flowers that smelled sweet.

"My mother likes these." She said.

We followed the stream, to where the water was blocked by rocks. A pool of water had formed behind them, and the trail went beside the pool

"There." she pointed to steps that led up to a hut.

The hut was surrounded by trees, and I thought of the medicine man camp, where the holy man took me as a boy. Many birds sang, and this place felt good.

"Come." Sael said, and we walked past the pool, to the hut.

"Mother!" she called.

I looked up, and saw a woman walk from inside the hut. As I got closer, I saw her more clearly. She had long hair, that fell in waves, down to her waist. It was dark, with streaks of light like the sun, when it shines on the water.

"Sael, who have you brought?" she said, and smiled.

I took a quick breath in when I saw her smile.

"Kai," Sael answered, "he is from another island."

We now stood at the bottom of the steps, and I looked up into her eyes. They were brown, and turned up at the sides.

"Welcome." she said, and smiled again.

Sael grabbed my hand, led me up the steps, and I stood looking down into her mother's face.

"Sit," she pointed to a log next to the doorway.

I sat, and she sat on a log beside me.

Sael handed her mother the flowers.

"Thank you!" She said, and put them to her nose, "they smell sweet."

She looked at me, "I like to smell them when I go to sleep."

"What is your name?" I asked.

She smiled again, "Autua."

"Why do you not live in the village?"

"My grandmother lived here after my grandfather passed," she looked at her daughter, "after Sael's father passed, we came to live here also."

"When did he pass?"

"When Sael was a baby."

"Where are your mother and father?" I asked.

"They live in the village, also my brothers and sisters."

"Yet you live here?"

She looked in my eyes, "My heart is quiet here."

I looked back into her eyes, and saw the brown was mixed with the color of plants.

"I have not seen hair or eyes such as you have."

"My grandmother had this color." she said, and held her hair in her hand.

I looked at her hair, and how it shined in the light. "I like it."

"Do you like my hair?" Sael asked, turned in a circle, so that her long dark hair swung around with her.

"Yes!" I said, and Sael smiled.

"Are you hungry?" Autua asked me.

I was not hungry, yet I wanted to stay here with her. "Yes."

SAEL SAT on the mat by our feet, and we ate fruit that Autua had picked. She asked me how I learned to make medicine, and I told her about the holy man. We spoke of much, and I did not see when Sael left, to play by the water.

"Sael!" Autua called to her, "bring water for tea."

I watched Sael fill a water pouch, and take it to a fire pit, built with rocks near the hut.

"I will start the fire." I told Autua.

"No," she said, "it is good for Sael to do it."

We watched Sael put twigs and dry leaves, on the hot wood in the fire pit. She used her hand to fan small flames, added more wood, then she put a water pot beside it.

Autua looked at me, "Sael knows how to live on her own. She gathers fruit, fishes, and can make a fire."

"You taught her?"

"Yes," she said, "she must be strong."

I looked at Sael, then back at Autua. "I know a woman that is strong, she is a warrior."

"I would like to see her."

"She is on the other side of the island, yet when she returns, I will bring her to you."

"Thank you." Autua said, and smiled again.

"I will show you the plants my grandmother used for medicine." Autua told me.

We walked down the steps, and behind the hut, where plants grew.

"I have used these." I said, "with mud on the skin."

She showed me others, and pointed to the plants they ate, and plants she used for tea.

"Will you show me other plants I can use for medicine?" I asked.

"Yes." Autua told me.

31

Sael carried the hot tea pot with a palm leaf, up the steps, and we followed her.

"My tea is good!" she said, and put the pot down.

"I will pour it." Autua told her.

We enjoyed our tea, and spoke of many things. I did not stop watching her as she talked. Her eyes, her smile, and her voice pulled me to her. I wondered if Konani felt this when he met Leilani.

The sun was behind the trees now, and I looked across from where we sat. Beside the trail, I thought I saw the holy man, then he was gone.

"He said this was my new home." I thought, and looked again at Autua.

CHAPTER 4

I waved to Autua and Sael, and walked back to the village. I
felt happy. I enjoyed Autua, I enjoyed seeing the plants her
grandmother used for medicines, and I enjoyed watching Sael play.
Her hut was shaded by trees, and made me think of the holy man's
camp. I breathed in the smell of the sweet flowers, and liked the sound
of water running in the stream. I wanted to go back, and I wanted to
see Autua again.

"Her smile." I thought, and saw her face.

"THERE WILL BE A FEAST THIS NIGHT!" Kekoa shouted to me, as I walked
to him. He stood on the sand, watching his warriors train young men
from the village.

"Good!" I said, and looked at his men.

"I will leave men here, to train the villagers." he told me.

I nodded, "We need warriors in each village."

Kekoa looked at me, "Will the men in the big boat come back?"

I looked at him, knowing he wanted me to ask the ancestors. I
closed my eyes, took in a breath, then blew it out slowly. I looked into
the darkness behind my eyes, and was quiet.

"The men on the big boat will not return," my teacher said, "yet the villagers must be prepared for others."

"We must prepare," I told him, "the boat will not return, yet others will come."

Kekoa nodded, "We will prepare."

At the feast, I looked for Autua and Sael, yet did not see them. I wondered if they could hear the shouts and laughter, of the villagers around the fire pit. After the feast, men put more wood into the fire pit, and the fire raised high into the darkness. We stepped back from the heat, and villagers sat further back on the sand. I looked around, then at Kekoa, who nodded at me.

I raised my arms in the air, and the villagers got quiet. I closed my eyes, took in a big breath, and slowly blew it out.

"Thank you Great Father for this night. Thank you Great Mother for the fish we eat, and the good water to drink."

I opened my eyes, looked at the villagers that sat in front of me, then closed my eyes again.

"Ancestors, thank you for protecting the village, and guiding us."

A holy man had not spoken in this village, and the villagers did not move.

"Ancestors come to our fire pit this night. Let us know you are with us."

I opened my eyes, and was happy to see many ancestors, standing amongst the villagers.

"Speak to your ancestors, they are here, and will listen to you." I told them.

Slowly the villagers started talking to those that had passed. I saw an old man sitting on a log by himself. Next to him, was a woman that shone with light, and I knew she wanted me to speak for her. I walked to the man.

"You sit by yourself?" I asked him.

He looked at me, "My children are here with their families."

"Has their mother passed?"

He nodded, "Yes."

I looked at her, and she put her hand on his shoulder.

"She is here with you."

He smiled, "I feel her."

I heard her say, she would be with him, when he passed.

"She said when you pass, she will welcome you."

"I will be happy to see her."

I put my hand on his shoulder, then left.

As I walked away, I thought of the holy man speaking with villagers such as this, yet I had not known why. The ancestors used him, and now me, to speak with their families.

I AWOKE on the sand under a palm tree, sat up, and looked at the water. It was smooth and clear over the sand, with the waves far away in the deep water. The sand stretched long between the rocks on each side of the village. I wondered why the waves did not crash on the sand close to the village, yet I liked the look of this smooth, clear water. I saw fish of many colors swimming in it. I wanted to swim here also, and feel my body in this water. I stood up and looked around, I saw Kekoa and his warriors still sleeping, further down the sand.

I stretched my arms up, swung them around, then ran into the water. It was warm, and the sand was soft under my feet. I ran until the water was deep, so I could dive in. My hair touched my back, as I swam under the water. I kicked my feet, and pulled with my arms, to move into the deeper water. I came up, and took a breath of air, "This feels good!"

I looked around, and enjoyed what I saw. Many palm trees grew, blowing with the wind, shading the huts, and along the trail that led through the village. I looked at the mountain, and thought of Autua.

"I will see her this day." I thought, "I will bring her food."

I swam to the rocks, and looked along them for shells.

"Yes!" Many shells grew on the rocks under the water, I pulled my blade from it's pouch, and started to cut them off. Suddenly I saw a large shell moving. I dove down, grabbed it from under a rock, and brought up the shell. It had a body as big as my hand, a shell that curled over it, and many legs coming out from under.

"This will be good!" I thought, and was careful not to let one of the legs pinch my hand.

I looked down, and saw that I had dropped the shells into the water, when I went after the big one.

"I will gather sea plants to eat with this." I thought, and gathered those. I walked out of the water holding the plants, and the large shell.

Kekoa stood on the sand, waiting for me.

"That will taste good!" he shouted.

I smiled, and called back, "I take these to a woman, and her daughter."

Kekoa raised his eyebrows, "Who is this?"

"Her name is Autua, and she lives by the mountain." I pointed up the trail.

Kekoa smiled big, "She is pretty to get such a feast."

I laughed, "She has shown me plants that I can use for medicine, so I will bring her food."

Kekoa laughed, "You have a good heart, yet I think she is pretty!"

I smiled, "I will take these to her, and make medicine today."

"I will train the villagers." he said, as I walked past him.

I grabbed my basket, put the shells in, then walked up the trail to Autua's hut. I waved to the villagers, as I passed, and wondered who was Autua's family.

I SMELLED sweet flowers as I walked by the stream, and picked some for Autua. I felt happy, and began to sing as I walked, and wondered if Sael played near her hut. I reached the pool of water, and looked up to the hut. It looked peaceful. As I got closer, I heard noise from the hut, it sounded like Sael crying out.

"She is hurt!" I ran up the steps, and stood in the doorway.

Autua sat on a mat next to Sael, rubbing her hand over Sael's forehead. Sael looked down, and wiped her eyes, as water fell from them.

"What is this?" I asked.

They both looked up. Autua's eyes were tired, and Sael's face was pinched in pain.

"Are you hurt?" I asked, and walked to look at her.

"Her mouth hurts." Autua said.

I put down the shell and flowers, raised Sael's chin, and felt her face was hot.

"Where does it hurt?"

Sael opened her mouth, put her little finger in, to point at a tooth in the back.

"Did you bite on a rock or shell?"

Sael shook her head, "No."

"She has not slept," Autua said, "the pain will not leave."

I had seen the holy man pull out an old man's tooth, yet I had not done this.

"Can I feel it?"

Sael nodded, I put my finger into her mouth, pushed on the tooth, and felt the skin in her mouth was hot also.

"Ohhh" she said, and more water fell from her eyes.

Autua put her arm around Sael, and looked at me. Autua's eyes asked me to help.

"I have no medicine for a tooth." I told her.

"I will take her to my father." Autua said, "he will help us."

Autua helped Sael to stand, I picked her up, and she lay her head on my shoulder. I felt the water from her eyes on my skin.

"I brought a large shell, " I told Autua, "and flowers."

She smiled, "He brought flowers!" she said to Sael. Sael looked at them, then lay her head back on my shoulder.

"I will put these in the water, while we are gone." Autua said.

I carried Sael, and followed Autua down the steps to the pool of water. She put the large shell, and sea plants, under the water. She looked at me and smiled,

"Thank you."

Autua led us to her mother and father's hut, in the village.

"Mother." Autua called, as we walked closer.

Her mother sat weaving, and looked up.

"Is Sael hurt?" she asked.

Sael lifted her head off my shoulder, looked at her grandmother, and cried out,

"Grandmother!"

"My baby!" her grandmother said, dropped her weaving, and walked quickly to us.

Sael reached out her arms to her grandmother, who took her from me.

"What is this?" said a man, now standing in the doorway of the hut.

"Sael's mouth hurts, she cannot eat or sleep." Autua said.

The man walked to his wife and Sael.

"Father, this is Kai." Autua said.

He looked at me, "The holy man at the fire pit."

Autua looked at me, yet I did not speak.

"Let me see your mouth." Sael's grandfather said, and put a finger in it.

"Ohhh," Sael cried.

He took his finger out, and looked at me, "You are a medicine man?"

"I have no medicine for this."

He bit his bottom lip, and looked at Sael.

"When I was a boy, my mother gave me the ceremony juice to drink," he said, "I fell asleep, and when I awoke she had pulled out my bad tooth."

"Can you do this?" Autua asked.

He nodded, "I have pulled out my brother's tooth."

I wondered how he pulled it out.

He looked at Sael, then back to Autua, "Get the strong juice."

Autua walked into the hut, and brought it out.

"Drink this." she told Sael.

Sael took the juice, and sipped.

"It is bad!" she said, and water fell from her eyes.

Sael's grandmother still held her, and turned her chin to look at her, "Drink."

Sael shook her head, then her grandmother took the juice, and put it to her mouth.

Sael closed her lips tight, and shook her head.

"Sael" Autua yelled.

Autua's father stepped up, grabbed Sael's face with his hand, and held the juice in the other.

"Open!" he told her.

Sael opened her mouth, and her grandfather slowly poured the juice into her mouth. Sael swallowed it, then he poured more into her mouth.

"When she sleeps." he said, and looked at Autua, "I will take out the bad tooth."

"I will help." Autua said, and wiped water from her eyes.

"Your mother will help," he told her, "we will care for Sael, and she will sleep in our hut this night."

Autua looked at Sael, who was still held by her grandmother. Water came into Autua's eyes.

"I will not leave!" she told him.

Her father put his hand on her shoulder, "Go rest."

Autua looked at her mother, who stood rocking Sael.

"She will sleep," her mother said, "after he takes out her tooth, we will give her more juice to sleep."

Autua's father spoke, "Come back when the sun rises, she will smile when she sees you."

Autua put her hand on Sael's hair, and leaned over to put her lips on her face.

"I will come back when the sun rises." Autua told Sael.

Sael nodded, and closed her eyes.

"Go," her mother said, "she will rest."

Autua turned, and walked away on the trail. I looked at Sael, then to her grandfather, "Can I help?"

"Care for Autua," he said, "I will care for Sael."

I nodded, and ran after her. She walked fast up the trail, I reached her, and grabbed her arm.

She turned to me with eyes full of water.

"You need rest." I told her

She nodded, and did not speak.

WHEN WE REACHED HER HUT, Autua sat on a step, and I sat next to her. We looked at the trees and sky.

"She feels Sael will leave her." my teacher whispered.

I turned to look at her, and she looked at me.

"I need.." Autua dropped her head, and her hair fell covering her face. I put my arm around her, and pulled her to me. I knew water fell from her eyes. She looked up at me, with water running down her face.

"She has been with me since her father passed."

I pushed her hair behind her ear, and looked into her eyes. I felt her sadness.

"Tell me what you need." I told her.

"Stay with me."

I smiled, "I will not leave."

She nodded.

"Will you eat?" I asked.

"Yes."

I stood, and walked away. She sat on the step, watched me gather wood, and start a fire. Then I soaked leaves in the pool of water, wrapped them around the large shell and the sea plants, and put them near the fire in the pit.

I walked back to Autua, and stood looking at her.

"Her father passed, I do not want her to pass also." she told me.

I wanted to say Sael would not pass, yet no words came.

"Your father and mother care for her," I said, "we will see her soon."

She nodded and took in a big breath, then let it out. "We will see her when the sun rises."

I walked away, and gathered more wood for the fire pit. I found a big log, and dragged it near the fire pit to sit on.

"We will sit by the fire this night!" I called to her.

She smiled, and watched me with a look I had not seen. I smelled the shells and sea plants, and knew they were ready to eat. I used sticks to lift the hot leaves out of the fire pit, laid them on a rock, and carefully opened the leaves. The sea plant was soft, and my mouth watered. I waved for Autua to come to the fire pit, and we sat on the log to eat. The meat from the shell was sweet, and the plants tasted like the sea water. I made tea, we sipped it, and watched the sun drop behind the trees.

"Night comes early here." she told me.

DARKNESS FELL AROUND US, I put my arm around her, and pulled her to me. She leaned against me, and we sat watching the fire burn. I looked at her, and she turned to look at me.

"I will..." I started to say, then leaned down, and put my lips on hers.

Her lips were soft, and I felt my body get warm. I pulled back to look at her again, and she put her hands on my face. She smiled at me, and slid her arms around my neck.

"Thank you." she said.

"Why do you say this?"

"I have been a mother, now I feel," she said, and looking into my eyes, "a woman again."

Autua dropped her hands, looked back at the fire, and we sat quietly. I looked down, and saw her hair falling against my arm. It looked soft, and I took it in my hand.

"I like your hair."

She turned to me, "Are you a holy man?"

"I am a medicine man."

"My father called you a holy man."

"I call the ancestors to the fire pit, and thank them for guidance."

"You speak to the ancestors?"

"Yes."

She smiled, "You are a holy man."

I still held her hair, and looked down at it in my hand.

"Why do you stay here?" I asked.

"I feel my grandmother here." she said, "and I wanted to stay away from the village."

"Why?"

"After Sael's father passed, his brother wanted to join with me."

I looked at her, yet she looked at the fire.

"My heart hurt," she said, "I did not want his brother, yet my father said to join with him.

"He wanted you to join with him?"

"I said no, and came here, to be with Sael in peace."

"Was your father angry?"

She shook her head, "He wanted the brother to care for me, yet he knew I was not ready."

We sat quietly, and I looked at her, she was still young.

"Will you join with another man?"

"As Sael has grown, I have cared for her, and not thought of caring for a man," She looked up at me, "Now I think of this."

"I think of this." I whispered to her, and put my lips on her forehead.

"Have you joined with a woman?"

"No."

Autua smiled, and put her hand on my leg, "I am tired."

WE STOOD, and she grabbed my hand. Autua led me inside the hut, and stopped. She let go my hand, and pulled the cloth that covered her body, up over her head. She stood in the moonlight, and showed me her soft body. Then she pulled at the rope that held the cloth at my waist, and it dropped to the ground. She put her hands on my chest, then ran them down to my legs, and I felt my body shake.

"You are strong." she said, wrapped her arms around me, and leaned her head on my chest.

I looked down at the top of her head, and lifted her up to me. I felt her body against mine, and I wanted her. She wrapped her legs around my waist, and her arms around my neck, then I carried her to the mat where we lay down.

"I will make you happy." she whispered to me.

CHAPTER 5

I awoke when the sun lit the inside of the hut, and looked
down at Autua, sleeping against me. She lay on her side
facing me, so close I only saw her hair spread out covering her arm
and the mat. She breathed softly, and I looked at her body. Her hip
was smooth, she had one leg bent, and it fell forward toward me. I put
my hand on her hip, and slowly ran it down her leg, thinking how we
had joined our bodies during the night. As I thought of this, my body
wanted to feel Autua again. I pushed the hair from her face, and
leaned down to put my lips on her neck. She moved as I put my lips to
her ear.

"You made me happy." I whispered to her.

She smiled, opened her eyes a little, to look at me from under her
lashes.

"You made me happy." she told me.

I pulled her to me, and squeezed. My body wanted her, my heart
wanted her, and I wanted her to be my woman.

"My heart has joined with her." I thought, and I wanted to tell her I
would protect her, and Sael.

I pushed her away, and her eyes opened wide.

"What is this?" she asked, as I held her away from me, looking into her eyes.

I took in a breath, and blew it out, "I thank the ancestors for bringing you to me."

She smiled.

"I want to be with you." I told her, and stopped to see her face, "I want to join with you."

Her eyes filled with water, and she brought her face close to mine, "I want to join with you."

As WE WALKED AWAY from Autua's hut, I looked back, and now saw this as my hut. I saw myself growing plants for medicine here, weaving baskets, and having a new life with Autua and Sael. I was happy, and knew that Autua was also. Now I knew how Konani felt, when he joined with Leilani. Thinking of Konani, made me want to live near him, yet I knew this would not be. I did not want to travel on the sea again, and I was happy to live on this new island with Autua. I began to sing, and she sang with me. I walked behind her, and enjoyed watching her body.

"I will build a bigger hut, and put more plants in the ground to make medicine."

"I am glad that you want to live up here." she told me, "I enjoy the peace of the mountain."

"It is like the old camp, where I lived with the holy man."

WE WALKED ON, and soon saw the huts of the village. Autua led me back to her father's hut, and walked ahead of me into it.

"What is this?" I heard her say.

I stepped beside her, and saw Sael laying still on a mat.

"I could not pull the tooth from her mouth." Autua's father said, "and she yelled all night, from it hurting."

Autua dropped to her knees, and bent over Sael. "Why does she not move?"

"I gave her more juice, so she could sleep."

A bad feeling came to me when I looked at Sael. She looked so small, and there was no color in her face. Autua looked up at me, then back at Sael. Autua shook her, and Sael made noises, yet did not open her eyes.

"She still sleeps from the juice." her father told us.

Autua shook her head, and put her hand on Sael's face. "She is hot."

I leaned down, and felt her face, "Yes." I said, and looked at her father, "she needs cold water."

He nodded and grabbed a water pouch, which he gave to me. I poured it on her face, and she turned her head from side to side. Autua shook her, and Sael opened her eyes.

"Sael! Wake up!" Autua called to her.

Sael looked at her mother with eyes that did not see, and fell back to sleep. Autua looked at me.

"We must wait for the juice to leave her body." I told her.

Autua's father walked out of the hut, and I stood to follow him.

"Her tooth is tight in her mouth." Sael's grandfather said, "I tried to wrap a string around it, and could not."

He looked at me, "I could not pull it out."

"I will look." I told him.

I walked back into the hut, squatted down, and lifted Sael's head up to the light.

"Her body is hot." I said, and felt her wet hair.

I opened her mouth to look in. "The skin has grown over the tooth" I told Autua, "it was not like this."

I put my finger in, and the skin was hot, "I will bring a sea plant to put in her mouth, and make tea for her when she wakes."

Autua looked at me with fear, "Heal her."

I stood and walked quickly out, then down to the water. I wanted the green plant that grew on the rocks under the water. I ran down the sand, until the rocks were near, then went into the water. I swam out to a big rock, and looked down,

"There!" I said to myself.

Just under the water was the soft, small plant that I wanted. I got my blade, and cut it from the rock. When my hand was full, I swam back, looking for Kekoa as I neared the sand. I did not see him, and ran back to the hut.

"Sᴀᴇʟ!" "Sael!" I heard Autua screaming.

I ran into the doorway, to see the back of Sael's head hitting the mat. Autua tried to hold her daughter's head, yet it moved by itself.

"Look at her eyes!" screamed Autua,.

I looked at Sael's eyes, and they were looking up, without blinking. I dropped down on my knees, and tried to hold her head, so it would not hit the mat. Her teeth bit down, and red water came from her mouth. I looked at Autua, then to her mother and father that stood watching.

"I have seen this before." Autua's mother said, "before my sister passed."

"No!" screamed Autua, "do not say this!"

Suddenly Sael's head dropped down, her eyes closed, and she lay still on the mat.

I still held her head, and put my hand on her shoulder. Her body burned with heat.

"Give me the water pouch!" I called out.

Autua's father handed it to me, and I again poured the cool water on Sael's hair and face. Sael turned her head from side to side, and made small noises, yet she did not wake. I opened her mouth, and put a little of the green plant, back on her bad tooth.

"How can I heal her? "I thought to my teacher.

"She will not be healed." my teacher said.

I looked at Autua, and felt her sadness as my own. I wanted to heal her daughter, so that Autua would be happy, and we could be a family.

"I will ask the ancestors for help." I told Autua, then left the hut, and walked up the trail to find a quiet place.

I stood under a tree, and looked up, "Can I not heal her?"

There was no answer. I felt the soft wind on my face, heard birds singing, and I became angry.

46

"Why?" I yelled.

"Why are you angry that Sael will live with her father?" My teacher said.

"Autua does not want her to pass!" I cried out.

"It is Sael that is ready to pass."

My head dropped, my shoulders slumped, and I felt water come into my eyes.

I wanted to say many things, yet I knew I could not heal her. I was not sad for Sael. I knew she would be happy living with her father, I was sad for Autua.

"What can I do?"

"Care for Autua." was the answer, as her father had also told me.

I saw how the ancestors led me to the woman I wanted to join with, when she would need me for strength.

"I will be a good man for Autua. Thank you for bringing me to her."

I WALKED BACK to the hut, not knowing what I would say to Autua, and her father and mother. When I returned to the hut, Autua had not moved from Sael. She sat rubbing Sael's arm, and speaking quietly to her.

"Where are your mother and father?"

"My father gets fish from my brother, my mother will return with my sister." she said without looking away from Sael.

I walked to her, and sat down. "Good."

"Will the ancestors heal her?" she asked, not looking at me.

I put my arms around her, yet did not answer.

She looked at me, "Will the ancestors heal her?"

I could not tell her the words that would tear at her heart, so I leaned forward to kiss her.

Autua pushed my arms away, "Tell me the ancestors will heal her!" she yelled.

I looked into her eyes, and felt the water falling from my own, "I cannot."

Autua shook her head, "No!" "No!"

I tried to put my hands on her shoulders, and she pushed them off. "They cannot take my Sael!"

I wanted to help her, I wanted to make her heart feel good, yet I did not know what to say.

"She will be with her father." I said gently.

She jumped to her feet, looking down at me, and I did not see my Autua. Her face was twisted with pain, and her eyes were angry.

"You are a medicine man! Yet you have no medicine for Sael!" she cried out, "my father said you are a holy man! Yet the ancestors will not heal her when you ask!"

I jumped to my feet, and went to her. She pounded her fists on my chest.

"Go! I do not want you here!" she yelled.

"Autua," I said quietly, "I want to help you."

She covered her face with her hands, started to shake, and fell down to her knees.

"I want to pass with her." she said, and turned to lie on her side next to Sael.

I could not breath, and my chest pounded.

"No!" I shouted, "your heart will heal."

She put her arm over Sael, and closed her eyes. "Leave me."

I STOOD LOOKING AT HER, then turned, and left the hut. I wanted to wait outside, yet I knew that Autua's mother and father would return soon. I did not want to speak with them now, so I walked behind the hut, and found a tree to lean against. I sat down, and felt my heart hurting in my chest.

"Autua, Autua..." I said softly, and water fell from my eyes, "We were happy."

I thought of sitting with her by the fire pit, and lying with her at night.

"We will be happy again." I told myself.

I listened to the sounds of the village. Far away I heard Kekoa's loud voice speaking, and laughing with his warriors. Then I heard Autua's mother and sister return to the hut, and was glad that she was not alone, yet I wanted to be with her also.

"She is angry that I cannot heal Sael!" I thought, and shook my head. "I cannot heal Sael, and I cannot help Autua."

I had helped my family, and many villagers, yet I could not help the woman I wanted to join with. My head hurt. I put my arms around my bent legs, and lay my head down. I sat quietly, feeling my head pound.

I heard Autua's father return, and smelled cooked fish. My belly was hungry, yet I did not move. My eyes were tired, and my body felt like I had run across the mountain. I thought of my mother's passing, and knew Autua's heart would heal as mine had.

"I will help her heal." I thought.

I sat listening to the voices of Autua's family, and villagers that came and went from the hut. Then stood, and walked to the stream where I met Sael.

"Thank you," I told her, "for bringing me to your mother."

I walked along the stream, back to Autua's hut, and saw it shaded by the mountain and trees. I went up the steps, looked inside at the mat where we slept, and wanted to feel close to Autua. I walked to it and sat, smelling the flowers I brought her. It was quiet, and I felt peace. I lay down and closed my eyes.

My body jerked, and suddenly I was awake. The sun had gone down, and light was leaving. I jumped up, and ran from the hut, down the trail to the village. As I got closer, I heard screaming, and knew it was Autua.

"She has passed." Autua's father told me, when I reached the hut.

Autua lay next to Sael, holding her, and calling out. "Do not leave me!"

The grandmother sat, leaning over, holding both her daughter and granddaughter. When I tried to sit with her, or touch her, she pushed me back. I could only watch as Autua screamed, and pounded her fists on the floor.

"Ancestors be with her," I thought, "help her heal."

I sat down in the hut, and darkness fell. Autua's mother and father lay on their mat, while Autua lay holding Sael. She had stopped screaming, yet she did not sleep. I heard noises coming from her, and knew her heart was broken.

CHAPTER 6

*A*fter Sael passed, her body was taken to the mountain, where her father was placed. Autua was helped by her mother and father, to walk up the mountain. I tried to walk with her, yet she shook her head, so I walked near her.

It was a peaceful place, and looked down on the sea. Stones were laid, then flowers were thrown over the stones. Autua's family, and the villagers, were sad and much water fell from their eyes. Autua looked at the stones, where her daughter lay, and no water fell from her eyes. Her arms hung down, and she did not move or speak. Autua's mother put her arm around her, and led her back to the village. I felt she had passed with Sael, and only her body stayed here.

"How can I care for her?" I asked my teacher.

"Stay close."

I watched Autua's mother and father care for her. I watched Autua's family come to see her, yet she did not speak.

"She does not want to live." I thought, and I heard others say this also.

She stayed in her father's hut for many suns, I slept in Autua's hut at night, then returned to sit under the tree to be close.

. . .

"WHAT IS THIS?" Kekoa asked as he walked to me.

I looked at him, and shook my head.

Kekoa squatted down next to me, "Why do you sit here?"

"I was to join with Autua."

"The girl's mother?" he asked.

Kekoa had been at the feast for Sael, and saw me walking to the burial site.

He slapped me on the arm, "I am happy for you."

"She will not join with me now." I said, and was sad.

"She will." he told me.

"I could not heal her daughter, and she is angry with me."

Kekoa squeezed my shoulder with his big hand, "Come! East some fish with me."

I looked at him, "I must stay close to her."

Kekoa nodded, "I will have a man bring you fish."

He stood and looked at me, "You need to eat!" then walked away.

My belly was hungry, and when Kekoa's warrior brought fish, I ate quickly.

"Thank you Kekoa." I thought, and leaned back against the tree, with a full belly.

THE SUN WAS RISING, as I walked down the trail, and heard Autua's mother.

"No! Stay here!" she yelled.

"We will care for you." Her father said.

Then I saw Autua walk out of the hut, she did not look at me as she passed by. I stopped, watching her walk up the trail to her grandmother's hut, then turned to her father.

He pointed to her, "Go."

I nodded, and I followed Autua.

I walked behind her on the trail, and watched her. She walked slowly, looking down at her feet. I heard her speaking quietly, yet did not know what she said. When we reached the pool of water, in front of her hut, she turned to me.

"Leave me." she said quietly.

I shook my head, "I will care for you."

She looked into my eyes, and stood up straight.

"I will care for myself." She turned, and walked away.

"I will watch over you." I thought, "your father and the ancestors want me to do this."

I took a step and thought, "You are my woman."

She walked up the steps to her hut, and went inside. I walked to the fire pit, and started to make a fire.

"We need to eat," and thought of what I would cook for us.

"Shells." I thought of the shells I found before, "I will gather those quickly, and return to watch over her."

I looked up and saw her watching me from the hut, so I smiled and waved. She stood watching, yet did not smile or wave, so I walked quickly down the trail away from the hut. The smell of sweet flowers stopped me.

"She will like these." I thought, and gathered some for her. I walked back to the hut, and saw Autua walking around behind it.

"Where does she go?"

I walked quickly to follow her. When I walked behind the hut, I did not see her, and looked from side to side. There was only the mountain here, which was steep and high, so I looked up.

"There!"

I saw Autua's long hair shining in the sun, as she climbed up the mountain.

I dropped the flowers, and started to climb after her. She was climbing fast, so I took long steps up the mountain. As I climbed, I looked up to the top of the mountain, and wondered why she would climb here. She reached the top, and stepped over where I could not see her. I ran, jumping over rocks, and reached the top.

"No!" I yelled.

She stood with her back to me, on the edge of a high cliff. She looked back at me, then turned her head to look away. As she lifted her foot into the air over the edge, I ran and jumped to reach her. I grabbed her with both arms, and pulled her back. We both fell on the ground.

"Why?" she screamed at me.

"My heart has joined with you." I screamed back, "you must live!"

"You will find another woman." She cried out, and tried to free herself from my arms.

"No!" I yelled, "You are my woman!"

Autua looked into my eyes, leaned her head back, and screamed loudly to Sael.

"Wait for me!"

I held her tightly, not wanting her to run back to the cliff. When she stopped screaming, she started to cry out loud, "Sael!" "Sael!" then water poured from her eyes, and she fell against me. I held her while she let the sadness pour from her.

"I am here." I whispered again and again.

I carried her down the mountain, and lay her on the mat in the hut. We did not eat this night, I feared leaving her. When I lay down beside her, I pulled her against me, wrapping my arms tightly around her. We lay quietly, I listened to her breath until she slept, then I closed my eyes.

"I WILL LIVE."

I opened my eyes, and Autua still lay wrapped in my arms, with her back to me.

"I will live for you." she spoke quietly.

I put my face in her hair, and water fell from my eyes.

Autua felt this, and turned to face me. She put her lips on mine, then leaned back to look at me.

"Thank you." I whispered.

She had great sadness in her face.

I looked into her eyes. "Will you join with me?"

She nodded, yet did not smile.

"I will help your heart heal," I told her, "I will not leave you."

I left the hut, made tea, and Autua sat on the steps.

"We will swim!" I yelled to her.

I brought her tea, and sat on the step beside her.

"We will swim." I said again, and looked at her.

She did not speak.

I put my arm around her shoulders, "I am here."

She leaned her head on my chest, and put her hand on my leg. "Thank you."

I gathered fruit, and we walked down the trail. I was happy that she walked beside me, now knowing why my teacher wanted me to stay close. If I had not, she would have passed to be with Sael.

We came to her mother and father's hut, and saw her mother weaving as we passed. Autua did not stop, when her mother looked at us, I waved to her. Her mother nodded to me, and I felt she was glad I watched over her daughter.

"I LIKE THE WATER HERE." I said, and put the fruit down, to grab Autua's hand. I pulled her with me to the water, we walked slowly into it, until it washed over our legs.

"It feels good." I told her.

I wrapped my arms around her, then fell back into the water.

"Kai!" she called out, as we went under.

We came up, and I pulled her to me, putting my lips on hers. She wrapped her legs around my waist, and put her arms around my neck. I stood in the water holding her, as the water gently rolled in around us.

"I like this village." I told her, looking back at it from the water.

"I want to leave," she said, "I want to live in Kekoa's village."

I pulled my head back to look at her. "You want to leave your mother and father?"

"I cannot live here."

I knew this village made her think of Sael. "We will live where you want."

She nodded.

"We will join before we leave." I told her.

"Yes," she said, "we will join."

"I am happy!" I said, and squeezed her tight.

We walked out of the water, and Kekoa stood watching and smiling.

I grabbed Autua's hand, and walked to him.

"This is Autua." I told him.

Autua looked at him, then back at me.

"We will be joined." I said.

"I am happy for you!" he clapped me on the arm, and smiled at Autua.

"She wants to live in your village."

"Good!" he said, "I am ready to go back."

I also wanted to go back. I wanted to build a hut, and start a new life with Autua.

"When will you join?" he asked.

"We will join this night." I said, looking into her eyes.

Kekoa nodded, "We will leave when the sun rises."

Kekoa left to prepare his warriors, and we left to see Autua's mother and father.

"We will join this night." she told them, and her mother wrapped her arms around Autua.

"He is a good man." her mother said, and let go to look at me.

"I will help you build a hut." her father told me.

Autua spoke, "We will leave when the sun rises, and go to his village."

"You will leave?" her mother asked.

I nodded, and Autua spoke again, "We will live there."

"Autua!" her mother cried out, "My granddaughter has passed, now you leave!"

"You have my sisters and brothers." Autua said, and held her mother's hands. Autua looked into her mother's eyes, "Sael and her father passed here, I will start a new life in Kai's village."

Her father nodded, "You will be happy there."

"You are welcome to stay with us." I told them.

"We will come to see your children!" her father said.

Autua's mother looked at her father, "We must prepare the feast."

"I will tell your sisters and brothers." her father said.

"I will go to my hut, and gather what I need." Autua told them.

"Go" her father said, "we will make a good feast."

We returned to Autua's hut, where she gathered a pot and a blanket. I took those from her, put them into my basket, and swung it over my shoulder. I walked from the hut down to the fire pit, and looked at this place where she lived.

"I will find a peaceful place such as this, to build a hut away from the villagers."

I looked up to see Autua walk out of the hut. She stood on the steps, wearing a cloth I had not seen. She wore a rope around her waist with a pouch hanging from it, and around her neck, was a string of shiny dark shells. My heart warmed, and I was glad I had found her.

"I am ready." she told me.

I walked to the bottom of the steps. "Come." and held out my hand.

She stepped to me, took my hand, and we walked away. At the pool of water, she stopped to see the hut again. Water came into her eyes, she bit her lip, "I will not return to this place."

She took in a big breath, blew it out, then turned and we walked toward our new life.

THE FEAST WAS GOOD. Many fish had been caught and cooked on the fire. Autua's mother prepared fish with fruit, and I thought of my mother making this fish, when I was a child. Autua and I sat together on a log, and were honored by the villagers with flowers and the ceremony drink. Autua's mother and sisters sang songs, villagers pounded on drums, and many villagers danced. I wanted to see Autua smile, yet she did not.

The song and dances were done, and I stood up. The villagers became quiet. I raised up my arms and took in a big breath, then blew it out while I dropped my arms.

"Thank you for this feast!" I called out, and the villagers shouted out.

"Thank you for the songs and the dance."

I looked at Autua, "Thank you for this woman that I will join with."

Kekoa and his warriors yelled, and laughed.

"We leave when the sun rises, and I ask the ancestors to guide us, and protect us."

I reached down to Autua, and took her hand to stand beside me. I looked into her eyes, she looked back and smiled. Not a big smile, yet I was happy to see it.

Autua's mother put a string of flowers over my head, then Autua's. Her father stood next to me, and he put his hand on my shoulder.

"Go!" he shouted for all the villagers to hear, "Join with my daughter, make many children!"

As we walked through the shouting villagers, they clapped us on the back, and threw flowers on our heads. We did not have a hut, so we walked away from the fire pit, along the sand by the water.

I looked up at the night sky, and it was clear. The moon was not big, yet it lit the sand where we walked. We walked to where the sand stopped, and rocks came down from the mountain. We looked back, saw flames from the fire pit, and heard the villagers, yet they were far away.

"Sit." I told her.

We sat down, and I put my arm around her.

"Are you sad to leave?" I asked.

She looked at me, "I am sad for Sael, yet I am happy to be with you."

"I am happy to be with you."

I put my lips on hers, and leaned her back on the sand. She wrapped her arms around my neck, and her legs around my waist. I leaned back to see her. Her hair spread out on the sand, and her eyes sparkled as they looked into mine.

I pushed her cloth up, and she pulled my cloth away. I felt her body against me, then we found each other, and moved together. She cried out, and grabbed my hair as she moved faster. I heard the water behind me, felt the wind gently blow across my body, and thought only of Autua. She pushed hard against me, then screamed and shook. I also pushed hard, and my water poured into her.

I fell back on the sand, breathing hard, and reached my hand over to lay on Autua's belly.

She sat up, "We will swim." she said, and pulled my hand to get up.

We walked into the water, washed our bodies, then swam under the night sky.

"I am glad we joined." I told her.

WHEN THE SUN ROSE, I opened my eyes. My arms were wrapped around Autua, as she lay with her back to me. We had put our cloths on the sand, and slept on top of them. I felt the sun on my skin, and raised up to look toward the village.

"Kekoa will be up." I thought.

Autua still slept, so I leaned down, and put my lips on her shoulder.

"Wake." I told her.

She made a noise, and started to move. I grabbed her hips, and pulled her back to me. She grabbed my hip, and pushed her body against mine. I joined with her again, and her screams came quickly. We washed in the water, put our cloths on, and walked back to the village.

"Are you ready to leave?" Kekoa asked when he saw us.

"Yes."

Autua's mother, father, and family were also there to see Autua before she left. Her mother gave her a basket she had woven, and her sisters had filled it with fruit and dried fish.

"Take this." her brother said, and gave me a small pouch with a hook and string for fishing.

"Thank you." I said, and clapped him on the arm.

Autua's sisters gave her strings of flowers for her neck, and strings of shells for her arms. We ate, and drank tea, while Autua spoke to her mother and father.

"We go!" Kekoa said loudly.

We stood and Autua's mother wrapped her arms around us. "Be happy." she said, and let go.

"Travel well." her father said.

The others reached out to touch our arms as we walked by, and told us, "Travel well."

WE CLIMBED to the top of the rocks, and Autua turned to look back on her village. Her mother and father still watched us, and she waved at them. I saw water come into her eyes, and I grabbed her hand. I waved to them, then we turned, and climbed down to the trail on the other side. Autua had not left her village, so I told her what she would see on the trail, and when we would get to Kekoa's village.

"Milana is there." I told her.

"You came from the old island with Milana?"

"Yes," I said, "Kekoa trained her to travel on the sea, and bring us back on the boat."

"Did he also train her to be a warrior?"

"Yes, and now she trains warriors."

"I have not seen a woman such as this."

I laughed, "There is no other!"

"Has she joined with a man?"

I shook my head, "She will not."

Autua looked at me, with her eyebrows pulled together, "She will not?"

"She does not want to care for a man or children."

"She does not want children?"

"She is happy to be a warrior, and a medicine woman."

"A medicine woman also?" Autua said, "I am glad we will live in this village."

"I am glad also. Milana is a sister to me."

We walked on the cliff trail, behind Kekoa and his warriors.

"Do you have a hut?" she asked me.

"No, I will build you a hut."

"Will we live in the village?"

"We will live where you want," I told her, and grabbed her hand, "I will build the hut away from the village, like your grandmother's hut, if you want."

She stopped, and turned to me, "I want that."

"I want you to be happy."

She smiled, "I am happy with you."

I smiled at her, yet knew her heart was not healed.

WE SPOKE of many things as we traveled. Autua said she would weave mats and baskets for us, and I told her of the hut I would build. She enjoyed seeing the island, and thinking of the new hut. I saw her eyes with water many times, and knew she thought of Sael, yet we did not speak of her. At night, we sat by the fire to eat, then Autua and I lay down on our bedroll. I wrapped my arms around her, and we slept.

I awoke in the night, and she was not on the blanket. I had not felt her leave my arms. I sat up, with fear in my heart, and looked around.

"Where is she?" I thought of the cliff not far away.

I jumped to my feet, then saw her walking back through the trees.

"Where did you go?"

"I went behind a tree." she whispered.

She stepped to me, and looked into my eyes, "I will not leave you."

I wrapped my arms around her, put my lips on her forehead, and was glad.

CHAPTER 7

*K*ekoa woke us when it was not yet light. "We must leave."

I rolled up our blanket, while Autua asked the men if they wanted fruit and dried fish from her basket.

"We will eat as we travel." Kekoa said, and he started down the trail.

We traveled until the sun was over our heads, sipping water from our pouches, and stretching our legs to keep us with Kekoa. Autua had stopped talking, and her breath came hard as she walked.

"Are you tired?" I asked her.

"No." she answered, yet I saw her face looked hot.

I stopped, and she did also. I grabbed my water pouch, poured water into my hands, and rubbed it across her face.

"Drink" I told her, she took the pouch and drank much.

"I know the trail," I told her, "we do not have to walk with Kekoa."

"When will we get to the village?" she asked.

"When the sun is low."

She looked at me, "Let Kekoa go ahead, I will walk with you."

I nodded, "We will enjoy our travel to your new village."

She smiled, "Yes."

I put my hands on the sides of my mouth, and yelled, "Go ahead!"

62

A warrior turned to look at me.

"We will see you in the village."

He nodded, and turned to walk behind the other men.

AUTUA and I enjoyed walking on the trail. We looked at the plants, I gathered tea leaves, while she gathered small fruits.

"Do you want that fruit by our hut?" I asked.

She nodded, "I dry these in the sun."

I looked for a small tree by its mother, dug it up with my blade, careful not to hurt the roots.

"I will put this in the ground by our hut." I told her.

She came over, and poured a little water on the dirt ball.

"It cannot dry," she said, "or it will not grow."

I watched her do this, "Do you enjoy growing plants?"

She looked at me, "Many plants, and flowers also."

"This is good," I told her, "I must grow many plants for medicine."

AS WE TRAVELED, I gathered plants for medicine and dug up a nut tree, which I also carried. The sun was going down, when we walked in the steep canyon, and we passed the stream of water that came down from the mountain. I looked ahead for the rocks on the trail.

"There!" I pointed to where large rocks covered the trail.

I walked to them, and took her basket, "Slide between the rock and the mountain."

She turned to the side, and slid through. Then I held her basket, my basket, and the trees above my head to slide through. She started to laugh when she saw me squeeze

through, while carrying so much.

"I am glad you are strong!" she said.

I had not seen her laugh since Sael passed, and it made me happy.

I handed her the basket she filled with fruit, and put mine on my back. I threw the trees over my shoulder, and pointed down the trail.

"The village is there."

"Good," she said, "I will be glad to stop."

Soon we saw huts under the palm trees, and looked to the sea. The air blew to us, and cooled our bodies. The sun was sitting on the water, and fish cooked on the fire pit.

"I smell fish!" I said.

"They smell good."

We walked between huts, and the villagers waved to us.

"Welcome!" they yelled.

I was glad to show Autua our new village.

"The villagers are happy." I told her.

The trail stopped at the fire pit by the water. Kekoa and his warriors stood by the fire, and many villagers also. They were eating, and enjoying Kekoa's stories, of the other village. They saw us as we walked to them

"Welcome!" a village elder called.

"Are you hungry?" Kekoa yelled.

I smiled, "Yes!"

I put down my basket and the small trees, then turned to take Autua's basket from her.

"We will eat." I told her.

I turned back to join Kekoa, and Milana stood in front of us.

"Welcome!" she said, and clapped my arm. She turned to Autua, "Welcome!"

I had not seen Milana wrap her arms around a man or woman, yet she stepped to Autua, wrapped her arms around her and let go.

"You are my sister, as Kai is my brother." she said, and looked at Autua.

I saw Autua looking at Milana with big eyes. Milana's body was strong, and had warrior markings. Milana looked back at Autua with a big smile.

"This is Milana." I told her.

"I am Autua."

"Kekoa told us of you!" Milana said.

"We are hungry." I told her.

. . .

MILANA WAS happy to tell me of the villagers she trained, and said she would help build our hut.

"You will sleep in my hut." she told us.

"Thank you." Autua said.

After we ate, the strong fruit juice was passed, I drank it and passed it to Autua. My belly was full, and my eyes tired, yet I wanted to say thanks. I stood up, and raised my arms. The villagers got quiet, and Kekoa spoke out, "Our holy man has come back!"

The villagers called out, "Yes!"

I raised my voice, "Great Father and Mother we thank you for the fish, and the fruit we eat. Ancestors we thank you for guiding us here safely. We ask you to join us."

The villagers called out, "Be with us!"

I looked down at Autua, saw water in her eyes, and I sat down next to her.

"I want my mother and father," I told her, "and Sael to see that we have joined."

She leaned her head against me, and water fell from her eyes. I put my arm around her, and leaned down, "We will go."

I looked at Milana, "We are tired."

Milana nodded and stood up, "Come with me."

I grabbed our baskets, the trees, and we followed Milana to her hut.

She pointed inside, "I will sleep in Kekoa's hut."

"Thank you." I told her, and brought Autua inside. I spread out our bedroll, and we lay down with my arms around her.

"Sleep well." I told her, and soon we both slept.

"Wake!" I heard Milana's voice, "We will eat, and build a hut this day!"

Autua and I sat up, and she rubbed her eyes. Her hair fell to the mat, with waves like the sea. The sun coming in the hut shined in her hair, like the sun shines on the water. I saw Milana looking at Autua's hair also.

"I like her hair." I said to Milana.

"I have not seen hair such as this."

Autua smiled, "My grandmother had this hair."

"Bring your hair to the fire pit and eat." Milana said, and walked out of the hut.

Autua looked at me, "I like her."

I laughed, "She likes you!"

"I WANT to build our hut by a stream," I told Kekoa as we ate, "where it comes from the mountain."

Kekoa nodded his head, and thought of this.

"There is a stream where the villagers get their water." Milana answered, "I will show you."

"I want to build the hut under trees, and away from the village.

"This is good." Kekoa said, "her screams will not wake the children!"

Autua took a quick breath, and I turned to look at her. She looked down, and her hair hid her face. The warriors laughed loudly, I looked at Kekoa, made a face and shook my head.

He shrugged his shoulders, "Your woman is happy, this is good."

"We will look for a place now." I said, grabbed Autua's hand, and led her away. We heard laughter, and the men talking as we left the fire pit.

Milana ran up behind us, laughing, "Kekoa likes you Autua! Do not be angry!"

"I am not angry," she stopped and looked at Milana, "I want a place where I can scream when I join with my man!"

Milana looked at her with an open mouth, then laughed loudly, and Autua joined her.

"Kai, I did not know you were such a man!" Milana said, and clapped me on the arm.

I laughed with them now, "I did not know!"

We walked up the trail, then Milana led us away under trees. Soon we heard water coming down the stream, and walked to it. Autua squatted down, and put water in her hand to drink.

"It is good." She said.

Milana and I also drank water.

"It is good!" I told them, "Where do the villagers fill their pouches?"

"Here." Milana answered.

"We will go up there." I pointed where the stream came down through the trees.

We walked along the stream, going up toward the mountain.

"Look!" Autua pointed to a large rock that stood high as me, with many trees around it.

"I like it." I said, and we walked to this rock.

A small plant grew over the stone, I reached out to touch it, and walked around the rock.

"Water!" I cried out. Behind the rock was water bubbling up from the ground. I squatted down, dug a hole in the dirt, and water began to fill it.

"This is good."

Autua looked at the water, then around, "We will build the hut there." She pointed toward the mountain, "where the dirt is dry."

"Make a pool to wash here." Milana said.

Autua led us to the area where she pointed. "The dirt is good. We can plant the trees, and grow many plants."

She smiled at us. "We have much to do."

We walked back to the village. Kekoa, his warriors, and many villagers wanted to help. Kekoa grabbed his long blade, then he and the others followed us back.

"I will make a pool to bath there," I said and pointed to where the water came up behind the rock, "we want to build the hut there." I pointed to the dry land.

He nodded, and looked at his warriors. "We will build your hut."

He pointed to the trees, "I will cut branches," he told his warriors, "you bring rocks."

Warriors gathered rocks to put at the bottom of the hut, then palm leaves and plants to put over the top. Villagers dug dirt, and put the small trees I carried back, into the ground. Kekoa cut branches and smoothed them with his long blade, then I pulled them to where we would build the hut. His warriors dug holes to put the branches in, and Kekoa looked at me. He wiped water from his face.

"Go," he said, "dig a pool so I can wash."

I DUG a big hole behind the large rock, and watched as the water filled it. I squatted down to wash my face and neck, then stood and looked around.

"The hut!" I was surprised to see it.

Kekoa and his warriors had shaped it with the rocks and branches. The top of the hut was being covered with palm leaves and plants, then tied down to the branches. I looked for Autua, and she worked with villagers, bent over putting plants into the dirt.

I was tired, and knew the men and women working must also be tired, yet I saw smiles.

I filled my pouch with water, and walked to them.

"Thank you" I told them, and gave them water to drink. I wanted them to know I was glad they helped. I had a new hut for Autua, a place where her heart would heal.

"I want her to be happy," I thought, "as I am."

I filled my water pouch again, and walked to where I would build the fire pit. It needed large rocks and logs around it, and I worked on this, until the sun was low.

"LOOK AT YOUR HUT!" shouted Kekoa.

"It is big!" I shouted back, and walked to it.

Autua walked out of the hut, and smiled at me, "It is big!"

I walked inside, and saw I could hang plants to dry, have many baskets for medicine, and room for many mats on the floor."

"Kekoa!" I called to him.

He walked in, stood next to me, and I looked at him. "Thank you, this is a good hut."

He laughed, "I made it big!"

I laughed, "You did, I do not need another hut for medicine."

Autua stood next to me. "Are you happy?" I asked her.

She nodded and smiled, "Thank you Kekoa."

I looked down at my feet, I stood on smooth branches that covered the rocks under.

"Water will run under the branches," Kekoa said, "your mats will stay dry."

"I have not seen this." I told him.

"On the island where I was a boy, we built our huts such as this." Kekoa pointed to the mountain by the hut, "Water will run down the mountain here."

"Yes," Autua said, "my grandmother's hut was built on rocks also."

Milana walked inside the hut, and looked at the long hut, "There is room for children!"

I grabbed Autua, and lifted her up, "We will have many!"

Autua laughed, "Let me make mats and baskets, then I will make a child!"

Milana and Kekoa laughed.

"Come," Kekoa told us, "we will eat in the village."

"Sleep in my hut." Milana said, "and make mats when the sun rises."

"Thank you." Autua said.

Kekoa and Milana walked out of the hut, and I stood with my arm on Autua's shoulders. She turned to look at me, and I knew she was happy. I smiled, and was glad that we had traveled away from her village, to build our hut here.

After returning to the village, we ate, then sat and enjoyed the fire pit.

Kekoa rubbed his eyes and stood, "I am tired!"

He left for his hut, and Autua looked at me with tired eyes.

I stood, looked at the warriors, the villagers and Milana, "Thank you for helping us. We will have a feast when the moon is big."

Milana stood, "Good!" then she walked away toward Kekoa's hut.

Autua and I walked to Milana's hut. We slept, and I dreamed of seeing Autua pour water on the plants by our hut. Then she turned to smile at me, and I saw her belly was full with child.

. . .

WHEN THE SUN ROSE, Autua and I went back to the fire pit.

"What will you do this day?" Kekoa asked.

"The hut is built, and the fire pit." I said looking at him, "we will make mats and baskets."

He nodded, "I will bring fish for your fire pit."

"Good!" I told him, "I will eat them!"

"Let Autua eat also!" he said, and laughed.

I looked at her, and saw that she was not soft as before. After Sael passed, Autua ate only a little, and the bones of her neck pushed under the skin now.

"I will." I said, and put my arm around her, feeling her small shoulders.

We walked to our hut, and sat down our baskets and blanket.

"It is big." she said, as we looked around, "I will make many mats."

"I will gather the palm leaves for you." I told her.

Autua nodded, "We will sleep here this night."

She put her arms around my waist, leaned against me, and I wrapped my arms around her.

"I will be glad to lay down with you."

I GATHERED MANY PALM LEAVES, pulling them back for a pile that Autua used.

"More?" I asked her, looking at the palm leaves stacked in front of her.

"Yes."

I walked back into the trees, and stopped to look around. She had much to work with, and I wanted to see what was around the hut. I found a stream, then followed it up toward the mountain. The trail we followed from the other side of the island, had come out near the village. In this area, the mountain was far back with the stream leading into it. I enjoyed the birds singing, and the gentle sound of water running over the rocks. There were many big bushes that grew large sweet smelling flowers.

"I will bring those back to Autua." I thought.

As I came closer to the mountain, I looked up seeing it reach into the sky. I saw a stream falling down from a cliff high above. The trees grew tall here and their branches spread out to cover my head. I walked by the stream, and now saw it blocked. Rocks, logs and bushes spread across the stream, yet the water found ways, to run under and through these. I walked beside this pile of rocks and logs and saw a big pool of water. The water did not look deep, yet it spread out along the bottom of the cliff. The waterfall filled this pool.

"Fish!" I looked around to see fish swimming in the water.

There was an area of dirt next to the pool, I walked to it, and saw small foot marks from birds that drank water here. A feeling of peace came over me, and I sat down on the dirt. I closed my eyes, and thought of when I was a boy sitting by the waterfall. I listened to the sounds around me, and breathed in the air.

"Have you gone away?" I asked my teacher, "You have not spoken to me."

I made my thoughts quiet, so that I could hear her.

"I have not gone away." she whispered.

"Why have you not spoken?"

"You walk your path," she said, "and learn much on your own."

"You are my teacher." I told her.

"I watch over you."

"I want to learn from you also."

"Many winds will blow over you. There will be warm, gentle winds and there will be cold, hard winds." she said.

I thought on this, "Good will come to me, and also bad. Are these the winds you speak of?"

"Yes."

"Yet you guide me?" I asked.

"I guide you to let the cold, hard wind leave your heart, so that the warm, gentle wind can come in to give you peace."

"Does not every man do this?" I asked.

"Some will hold the cold wind in their heart, feel angry and do bad."

"The big boat carried such men." I said.

"Yes."

"Do they not have teachers to guide them?"

"They have teachers, yet they will not hear them."

"My heart is sad for them." I told her.

"You learn well."

I felt my teacher's hand brush my shoulder, then she left.

I opened my eyes, "Thank you."

CHAPTER 8

I carried the small pouch with fish hook and string, that
Autua's brother gave me, so I pulled it out to fish. I put a
little wet plant on the hook, walked into the water, and threw it in. I
stood very still and gently pulled the string along in the water, while
looking around. On the side of the cliff, a large bird perched on a
rock.

"He must eat fish from this pool." I thought.

A small pull on my string brought my eyes back to the water. I
gently pulled the string to me.

"There it is!"

A fish came with the string back to me. Its tail moved from side to
side, and I knew that it fought against my hook. I pulled it out of the
water on to the dirt, and looked at it. It was as big as my hand.

"Thank you." I said to the fish.

I took the hook from its mouth, and lay it down on the dirt. Then I
put more wet plant on the hook, and walked back into the water. I
stood still, while I gently pulled the string. Suddenly I heard wings
flapping behind me. I turned to see the large bird picking up the fish I
caught, and flying up into the air.

"Bird!" I yelled at it.

It flew back to the rock, then leaned its head into a hole between the rocks.

"She feeds her babies!"

I watched the bird turn around, sit on the rock again, and look down.

"I will not fish for you!" I called out, then pulled my string and hook from the water, and walked out of the water.

"I will bring back a basket for my fish!"

I gathered more palm leaves, and the flowers, before walking to the hut.

"AUTUA!"

She walked from the hut, and waved for me to come.

I threw the palm leaves on the pile, then walked to her with the flowers.

"Thank you!" she said, took my hand, and led me into the hut.

I followed her into the hut, where the branches on the floor were covered, with a large mat.

I walked on it and turned to her. "This is good!"

She smiled, "I will make a mat to sleep on, and put our bedroll on it."

I smiled, thinking this night we would sleep here.

"I followed the stream, and at the mountain, there is a good pool of water."

"I want to see this." she said.

"Fish are in the water." I said, and told her of the large bird that I fished for.

Autua laughed, "You fed her babies, she will be happy to see you!"

AUTUA STAYED in the hut weaving mats, and I walked outside around the hut, looking at the rocks around the bottom. Mud had been packed between them, and after it had dried, there were some holes. I pushed more mud, and small rocks, into these holes. I also looked at the sides of the hut, and pushed against it with my hand.

"This is strong." I looked at how the big palm leaves, lay on thick small plants, over the branches. These had been woven tightly together.

"We will stay dry." I thought.

I looked at the dirt where the villagers had put the trees, and where Autua had put plants to grow. It looked dry, so I filled my pouch, and poured water on them.

"Kai!"

I looked to see Kekoa walking to me.

"Welcome!" I called out.

Kekoa stopped, looked at the hut and the plants I put water on, and nodded.

"Here!" he gave me the basket he carried.

I looked in to see many fish. "Thank you."

Autua walked to us, and looked in the basket. "Are you hungry?"

Kekoa shook his head, "I will go back."

I looked at him.

"Milana and I will travel around the island when the sun rises." he told me, "we will see the warriors that watch for the big boat."

I thought of walking on the trails, seeing the island, and gathering plants for medicine.

"Tell Milana to gather plants for medicine." I said, "I will bring her a basket."

"Bring it this night!" he said, and clapped me on the arm, "she will carry the basket and spears!"

"I will weave it now!" I told him.

"Good!" Kekoa said, and turned to walk down the trail to the village.

Autua followed me to the pile of palm leaves, and I sat down.

She watched me start to weave. "Will you travel to gather plants?"

I looked at her, "When I travel, you will travel with me."

She smiled, "Good."

. . .

75

AUTUA COVERED the bottom of the hut with mats, then used a palm leaf to push dirt from the hut. She wove a mat to sleep on from a soft plant, and put our blanket on it. And she lay the sweet-smelling flowers I brought her, down by our sleeping mat.

"I do not want to go!" I told her when I saw this.

"We will run back!" she said.

I put the basket I made for Milana on my back, grabbed Autua's hand, and we walked from our hut. We walked past the big rock, saw the large hole I dug, was filled with water and running out around the rock.

"I will dig more, and make a bigger pool!" I told her.

"I will wash there." Autua said.

"The ancestors have blessed us!" I said.

"THANK YOU." Milana said, and took the basket. She held it out, and turned it around.

"My spears go here!" she said, and pointed to the loops on both sides.

I smiled, "I made it to hold your spears, and many plants."

"Yes, it is big." she said, and slipped it on her shoulders.

"When you travel on the mountain," I told her, "bring me leaves for tea."

"I will gather many plants for you!" she said.

"Thank you." I looked at the sun sitting on the water, "We will go."

Milana looked at Autua, then me and smiled. "I will see your hut when I return."

I put my hand on her shoulder, "Travel well."

I followed Autua up the trail, and when she reached the big rock, she stopped.

"I will wash." She pulled the cloth over her head, I looked at her body, and was happy we would join this night.

"I will also." I told her, and dropped my cloth down.

Autua sat on the edge of the water, and put her legs in, then slipped down into it. She put her head under the water, and came up.

"It is cold!"

She grabbed her arm, and I pulled her out.

"I will bring rocks here to help us climb out." I told her, then got into the water.

It was cold, yet it felt good on my body, and I washed the dirt away. I put my head under the water, and got out of the pool. Autua stood, holding both our cloths.

"I will wash these."

She put them into the water, and rubbed them between her hands. When she finished, she twisted the water from them, hung them from a tree branch and turned to smile at me. The sky was getting dark now, and I saw her wet skin looked cold. I picked her up, she laughed, and I ran with her in my arms to the hut. I walked into the hut, and lay her on the sleeping mat. She lay on her back looking up at me.

"This is my woman," I thought, "and this is my new hut."

I felt happy, and smiled at her. "We will make a child."

AUTUA WORKED HARD when the sun rose. She filled the hut with mats, baskets, and plants hung up to dry. She put water on the plants and the small trees.

"You work hard!" I said.

"I am tired." she said, "I want to swim."

"I will take you to the waterfall I found."

We walked to the pool of water at the bottom of the mountain, and gathered feathers that fell from the mother bird by the pool. We put them in our basket, then went into the water.

"This is good!" Autua said, and went under the water.

I also put my head under the water, then lay on my back in it.

"I am happy." I told Autua as she swam to me.

"I am happy also." she said

I knew she thought of Sael much, and had seen water fall from her eyes. I raised my head, and looked at her. Her long hair was full of water, and it stuck to her.

"Thank you for joining with me." I told her.

She leaned over me, smiled, then pushed me down under the water.

I came up blowing water out of my mouth, and looked at her. She ran away from me. I quickly jumped up, and took long steps to catch her. Autua screamed as I picked her up, and put her over my shoulder. I walked to the waterfall, then under it. The water pounded on my head and her back.

"Ouch!" she cried out and laughed.

I put her down, she ran out from under the waterfall, turned and looked at me.

"Catch me fish!" she said.

I took the small hook and string from my pouch, prepared the hook, then threw it in the water. Autua sat on the dirt by the pool, and each fish I caught, she put in the basket.

"Are you ready?" I asked.

She nodded and stood up, then took a fish from the basket and put in on the dirt.

"For the mother." she said, and looked up to the bird sitting on the cliff.

I looked up at the bird, "She likes you!"

WE WALKED BACK to the hut, and I started a fire. Autua gave me the fish, then took the feathers from the basket, and washed them in water. She lay them on rocks to dry.

"I will use the big one for smoke at ceremonies." I said.

Autua gathered plants to eat with the fish, and we sat on the log by the fire pit.

"I like this fish!" she said.

"It is good!" I told her.

We drank tea, watched the fire, and the night slowly came down on us.

"Do you think of your mother and sisters?" I asked, thinking I would like to see Konani.

She was quiet, then, "I think of Sael."

I put my arm around her shoulder, and pulled her close to me. "I know."

I DUG out more dirt from behind the big rock, and made the pool larger. I carried big rocks to the hole, and put them in the hole to sit on, and around it so Autua could pull herself out. I thought the water would soon fill this large hole, so I dug a way for it to flow down to the stream.

"This is good." I thought as I looked at it.

Trees shaded the water, making it look dark, and the water was cool.

"We will enjoy this after we have worked, and our bodies are hot."

Autua walked to me, and looked at it. "I like this pool!"

I nodded, and was glad that I made her happy.

MANY SUNS ROSE, and each day Autua and I gathered plants. We put them in the dirt to grow, hung them in the hut to dry, and I put others in pouches for my medicine basket. We fished from the large pool by the waterfall, and got fish from the men that took boats out in the sea. I made Autua sandals, and she wove a thin string with a shell hanging on it. Autua tied it around my neck, and stood back to look at it.

"I like it." she said.

I reached up to touch the shell, and thought of the holy man touching the clear stone that hung around his neck.

"Thank you, I will not take this off."

Autua looked down at her new sandals. "I will not take these off!"

She smiled at me, "I will sleep with them!"

I laughed, grabbed at her, and she jumped back.

"I will not take them off!" She said, and ran from me.

I chased her, picked her up, and carried her into the hut.

"Do not take them off!" I told her, and laughed.

When we finished working each day, we washed in the pool by the big rock, put fish in the fire pit to cook, and spoke of many things as we sat by the fire in the darkness. She told me of Sael's father, who she grew with as a child. She spoke of joining with him, and of bringing in his Sael. Then she spoke quietly,

"He fell from wet rocks, hit his head, and went into the sea." she told me, "his brother swam to him, and brought him to the sand, yet he had passed."

"You are a strong woman." I told her.

"I had to care for Sael."

I held her close to me, and we watched the flames in the fire grow small, leaving the hot wood at the bottom.

"Are you tired?" I asked.

She looked up at me and smiled, "No."

I had been happy when I lived with the holy man and Konani, yet I had not felt the great happiness I felt with Autua . My heart is full. My eyes are happy to see her, and my body glad to feel her.

As we talk and I know more of her, I thank the ancestors that such a woman joined with me. She was happy also, and her body was soft again, from eating much fish and fruit with me.

"Thank you for this peace." I thought.

"Enjoy." my teacher whispered.

LIGHT CAME INTO THE HUT, and I rolled over to see Autua. She lay on her back, with one arm out to the side, and her long hair covering most of her chest. I watched her breath, and leaned the side of my head over to feel the air, as it came from her mouth. Suddenly I felt her teeth on my ear.

"No!" I cried out, and she bit my ear, yet it did not hurt.

I put my leg over her body, and grabbed her arms.

"I will bite you!" I said, and put my head into her neck.

Autua screamed and laughed, and tried to move away. I put my lips on her skin, then leaned back to see her. She had stopped fighting, and looked at me with a small smile. I put my lips on her shoulder, moved my mouth down along her skin, and she moved her hips under me. We joined much now, and the birds answered when they heard

Autua's screams. She thought a baby would heal her heart, and many times Autua pulled me to her. I was happy to join with her, and wondered what my child would look like.

AUTUA and I walked to the village to get fish, and to give medicine to the villagers. Kekoa and Milana had not returned, and I wondered what they saw as they traveled around the island. Autua spoke with an old woman, then came to me.

"I grow a child." she said.

I looked at her, and she spoke again, "I grow a child." then she rubbed her belly.

I grabbed her up, lifting her off the dirt. Water filled my eyes, yet I was happy.

"When will the child come?" I asked.

"After many big moons."

I yelled out, "I will be a father!" and many villagers laughed and smiled.

CHAPTER 9

*K*ekoa and Milana returned to the village, and Kekoa
sent one of his warriors to me.

"He wants you to join him at the fire pit this night."

"Tell him we will."

The warrior left, and I turned to Autua, "We go to the village."

She nodded, "I will speak to the old woman of the baby."

"Is it good?" I asked.

"My breasts hurt as they grow," she told me, "as they did when Sael
grew in me."

I looked at her breasts, and they had grown.

"I like them." I told her, and reached toward her.

Autua laughed and jumped back. "They baby will like them also!"

WHEN THE SUN went behind the trees, we left our hut. We took our
baskets, mine with medicines, and hers was empty to fill with fish and
fruit from the village.

I followed Autua down the path, and looked at her long hair move
as she walked. I wondered if our baby would have her hair, with
waves, and streaks of sun in it. I looked over her head when I heard

Kekoa's voice. He spoke loudly at the fire pit, yet I could not hear what he said.

Autua stopped in front of the old woman's hut, "I go here."

I leaned over and put my lips her on the head, then she walked away from me.

I walked down to the fire pit, and sat my basket down. Kekoa saw me and came over.

"Welcome!" he shouted, and clapped me on the arm.

Milana joined us, and we sat on a log. She passed me a shell with the strong juice.

I smelled it, "It is strong!"

Kekoa and Milana both laughed, "Yes!"

While I sipped it, Kekoa spoke. "The warriors have not seen a big boat."

"They want to stop watching, and come back to the village." Milana said.

I shook my head, "We must have warriors watching the sea."

Kekoa and Milana listened.

"There will be a boat that comes," I told them, "bad men from another island, or sickness will come to kill our villagers."

Kekoa shook his head, "We will train our warriors to be strong," he turned to looked at Milana, "we will watch for the boat."

Milana nodded. "I will train more men, and take them to watch for it."

"Good," Kekoa said, "these young warriors must be prepared."

"The villagers also need to be prepared." I said.

Kekoa stood up, "I will take my warriors, and the village men, to build huts on the mountain by the waterfall."

"Then the villagers can see where they must go." I said.

Milana and I both stood up, and Kekoa looked at me, "Ask the ancestors to help us."

I nodded, took in a big breath, and blew it out. I closed my eyes and held my arms up.

"Ancestors!" I called out, and the villagers around the fire pit got quiet.

"Guide us and protect us." I said.

Kekoa shouted out, "Help us prepare!"

"Thank you for being with us." I dropped my arms and opened my eyes. I saw many ancestors standing next to the people around the fire pit.

"Speak to your ancestors!" I told the villagers and warriors.

Then many begin to talk to their family that had passed. I looked at Kekoa, and saw a beautiful woman standing next to him, and felt it was his mother.

"Kekoa," I said quietly, and he looked at me.

"Your mother is here, she wants to speak with you."

He looked at me, not moving.

"Go." I said, and pointed to the dark sand by the water.

I watched him walk away to the water, and saw that his mother moved with him.

"Is my grandfather here?" Milana asked. I looked, yet did not see him.

"Find a quiet place, and call him." I told her, "He will come, yet he may not show himself. Talk to him, and he will hear what you say."

She nodded, and walked away toward trees in the darkness.

I looked at the villagers around the fire pit, and the ancestors that listened to them.

"Mother." I whispered, "be with Autua when she brings our baby in."

"She will be there." I heard my teacher say, "and many others."

This made my heart feel good, yet I wanted to know more. "Who will be there?"

"Autua's teacher, and your baby's teacher."

"My baby's teacher?"

"Your daughter has many that will protect her."

"My daughter!" I cried out with great happiness.

MANY BIG MOONS LATER, when Autua's large belly began to move and cause her pain, I took her in the night to the village. The old woman, and other village women, helped Autua. I waited outside, and heard her screams.

"Help her." I said again and again to my mother, and the ancestors.

Kekoa and Milana sat with me, and we drank the strong fruit juice as we waited.

"My woman has brought in many children," he told me, "mothers are strong like warriors."

I looked at Milana. She was quiet, and when we heard Autua scream, I knew she feared for her. I knew many young mothers had passed bringing in babies, and I also had fear. Our baby pushed her way out, just as the sun rose over the mountain, and she screamed loudly.

"She screams," the old woman told me, "this is good."

I walked into the hut and saw Autua, holding our daughter, now quiet. Autua looked tired, yet smiled and was happy.

"Her name is Halia." she told me.

I smiled and nodded. Water came to my eyes, as I looked down at my child. I had wondered what she would look like, and now I saw her. She had light skin like Autua, yet I did not see hair. I reached to touch her head.

"My mother said I did not have hair when I was a baby." Autua told me.

"I feel hair," I said as I rubbed Halia's head, "the color is light like yours."

AUTUA'S BREASTS WERE FULL, and our daughter drank many times during the day and night.

"I will make a bed for her." Autua said.

I looked down at our daughter sleeping between us. Every night Autua put many leaves, and the soft plants that grow on the rocks, under Halia. When the sun rose, Autua took these, wet with Halia's water, out to burn in the fire pit.

"She is protected here." I told her.

Autua smiled, "She will sleep there." and she pointed to the area between herself, and the hut. "I will sleep here." and she touched my chest.

I smiled, happy that Autua wanted to be close to me.

Autua washed Halia in the water by the big rock, let her drink, then sleep in her arms until she was dry. I followed Autua as she cared for our daughter, learning what was needed for a baby.

"Did your mother teach you this?" I asked.

"I watched mother care for my brothers and sisters."

"Halia is well cared for." I told her.

Autua smiled, and put her hand on Halia's head. "Feel this." she told me.

I reached over to Halia's head, and under my hand was soft hair. I pulled my hand away and looked closely.

"She has hair!"

"Look at her eyes." Autua told me.

I looked at Halia, her eyes went up at the sides. "Her eyes are like yours!"

We sat in the sun until we got hot, then moved to the shade, where Autua put a mat for Halia to sleep.

"We are blessed." I told her. Autua lay Halia down on the mat, then turned to me.

"We will be blessed with many children."

"Have you seen this?" I asked.

"The old woman in the village saw me having many babies with you."

"Good." I said.

"She said our son will be a great warrior."

"A warrior?"

"She said he will have many warriors that follow him," and Autua looked into my eyes, "he will be Alii on this island."

I put my eyebrows together, thinking of this. "Alli? I will speak to her of this."

.   .   .

WE SAT ON THE MAT, talking and watching Halia sleep, when we saw a warrior running up the trail.

I stood and walked to him, "Welcome!"

He stopped and put his hands on his hips, leaning over to take in big breaths.

I waited for him to speak, then he stood up.

"Kekoa asks you to bring medicine."

"Is he sick?"

"No."

"Tell him I will come."

The warrior nodded.

"Do you want water?" I asked.

"No," he said, showing me his pouch, "I have water."

Then he turned, and ran back down the trail.

I walked back to Autua, and sat down. "Kekoa wants medicine for his warriors."

"We will go, and see the old woman." she said.

"I want to hear of my son." I told her.

Autua carried Halia in a cloth over her chest, and carried a basket on her back. I carried my basket filled with medicines, and many plants. We walked into the village and Autua walked to the old woman, sitting in front of her hut. I walked down to the sand, where Kekoa stood, watching Milana train the warriors.

"You traveled fast." he said.

"Is a warrior sick?" I asked.

"No, I want to travel with medicines," Kekoa said, "and be prepared."

I was glad they were not sick, "I will give them medicines," I told him, "Milana knows medicines also."

Kekoa looked at me, "She has trained many warriors."

I looked at her, saw Milana throw a large warrior down to the sand, and sit on his belly holding a blade to his throat.

"I would not want to fight her!" I told Kekoa.

"She is stronger now." he said.

Kekoa yelled at the warriors, "Run, then swim."

We watched them run along the sand, and Milana joined us.

"You train well." Kekoa told her, "pick warriors to help you train the men."

She nodded and breathed hard.

"I will." Milana said, and looked at me, "You have come down from your hut!"

I laughed, "I have brought medicine for the warriors."

"Good," she said, "I will travel soon."

She looked at Kekoa, then me, "When will you travel?"

I pushed my shoulders up, "I do not know."

"You are a medicine man!" she said, "not yet old!"

"You are a medicine woman!"

I looked at Kekoa.

"She cannot make medicine now," he told me, "she trains."

"You do not want to leave Autua and Halia." Milana said.

Kekoa looked at her, "He will travel when the ancestors tell him."

I looked at Milana, "I will travel soon."

"Good." she said, then turned and walked toward the warriors' hut.

I watched her walk away, and looked at Kekoa.

"She feels her brother has left her." Kekoa told me.

I knew that I had left her. I left to be with Autua, and now Halia. I did not see Milana as I did on our home island, and my heart hurt that she was angry.

"I will talk to her." I said, "can she come to my hut?"

"She can come," Kekoa said, "yet she will not."

I nodded, "Tell her I took the medicine back to my hut."

Kekoa laughed loud, "You said you did not want to fight her!"

I laughed also, "She will be angry!"

I picked up my basket, and put it on my shoulders. "You are my brother, as Milana is my sister."

Kekoa grabbed my shoulders with his strong hands, "My little brother!" and let go.

"Milana must come to my hut!" I told him, and left with the medicine.

. . .

AUTUA SAT with the old woman outside her hut. Halia lay on the old woman's legs looking up at her. The old woman held her little hands, and spoke softly to her. When she heard me walking to them, she looked up.

"Welcome."

I walked to them and stopped. "You told Autua we would have many babies?"

The old woman smiled, and looked down at Halia, "This is a beautiful daughter."

"We will have a son that is a great warrior?"

The old woman looked up at me, "Come and I will tell you of this."

She put Halia on her chest and stood up, then passed her to Autua. She walked into her hut, Autua followed and sat on a mat in the corner. I walked behind into the dark hut, and looked around.

"Here." the old woman pointed to a mat, then she sat down.

I sat down across from her, and she looked at me.

"Give me your shell." she said, and pointed to the shell that hung from my neck.

I pulled it over my head, and passed it to her. She closed her eyes and held the shell, rolling it between her fingers, then passing it to the other hand.

I looked at Autua, she nodded, then back at the old woman. In the darkness behind her, I saw an ancestor standing.

"Her teacher." I thought.

I heard the old woman take a deep breath, then blow it out.

"Your son will be a warrior, and train many others to follow him."

I watched the old woman and her teacher.

"He will fight many to be Alli." she said, "and much blood will pour on the sands where he travels."

I thought of the chief's son that wanted to fight other villages. I did not want a son such as this.

"Must he do this?" I asked.

She nodded, "It is his path."

I pulled my eyebrows together, thinking how I would have him be a medicine man, not a warrior.

89

"This island will be his," she said, "you can teach him to ask the ancestors for protection."

She opened her eyes. "You are blessed." she said, and stood up.

I still sat, watching her walk to Autua, and take Halia in her arms again. The women walked outside, yet I could not move.

"Will my son be a man that fights to be alli?" I asked my teacher.

There was no answer, and I shook my head, "I will enjoy my peace now!"

MILANA WALKED with strong steps up the trail to our hut. I stood in front of the new plants I had put in the dirt, and watched her come up the hill. She swung her arms and looked down, and I felt her anger from where I stood. When she reached the clearing in front of the hut, I yelled to her.

"Milana!"

She looked at me, did not smile, and walked to me.

"Welcome!" I called out.

She stood back and looked at me, "Why did you bring me here?"

"You are my sister," I said, "you have not come."

She looked away from me, "I train the warriors, and travel around the island."

I looked up to see Autua standing in front of the hut, holding Halia.

"Come see my daughter." I said and stepped to her, putting my arm over her shoulder.

She looked up at me with angry eyes.

"You are a warrior," I told her, "yet you are still my little sister!"

I grabbed her around her arms and picked her up, then set her down on the ground. She smiled a little, and shook her head, then walked to Autua.

"Welcome." Autua told her.

Halia held her head up, and turned to see Milana. Her hair now stood up on her head, and grew in circles around her neck and face. Halia looked at Milana and smiled.

"She smiled!" cried Milana.

"Yes!" Autua said, and held Halia out to Milana.

"I.." Milana started to speak, when Halia held her arms out to Milana. Milana took the baby in her arms, and held her away from her body, looking at her.

Autua laughed, "Hold her like this." and showed Milana how to hold the baby.

Milana moved Halia to lean against her chest, and looked at her. Halia saw me and smiled.

"Haaalia." I whispered to her, she smiled and made noises.

"She is beautiful!" Milana said, and kept her eyes on Halia.

"Are you hungry?" Autua asked.

Milana looked at Autua, "I am."

"Go there" Autua pointed to the mat under a big tree, "I will bring food."

Milana and I walked to the mat, I took Halia and laid her on the mat, then we sat down.

"She watches the birds." Milana said, looking at Halia's eyes follow the birds.

"Come see her," I said, "or she will be a woman, and not know her father's sister."

Milana looked at me, "I did not know I was welcome."

I looked her in the eyes, "You are my sister, you are Autua's sister." I pointed to the hut, "This is also your hut, and Halia is your family."

Milana looked down at Halia, and reached out to touch her hair.

"She has her mother's hair."

Autua brought food, and Milana watched as Halia drank from her mother. We ate, talked, and laughed much.

"When you left the fire pit, did you see your grandfather?" I asked Milana.

She shook her head, "No, yet I felt him by me, so I spoke to him."

"Good." I told her.

Milana looked at Autua, "Do you feel your daughter that passed?"

I looked at Autua, and wondered what she would say. I had not asked her this.

Autua nodded, "I feel her much." then she looked at me. "Halia sees her."

"How do you know this?" Milana asked.

"When I feel Sael, Halia looks at her and smiles. She has done this much."

This made me happy, "Our daughter can see the ancestors!" I said.

"She is like her father!" Milana said.

Halia pulled away from Autua, and rubbed her face against her mother's chest. Autua moved her up, to look over her shoulder, and gently pounded Halia's back. Halia made a noise, and Milana laughed. Halia turned her head to lay on Autua's shoulder, and closed her eyes. Autua gently patted her back, and looked at Milana.

"Will you have a baby?"

"No, I am a warrior," Milana said, and looked at me, "and a medicine woman."

Autua looked at her and smiled. "You have much to teach a child."

"I will teach Halia." Milana told her.

"I would like that." Autua said, then lay Halia down on the mat to sleep.

"I will show you the plants I grow for medicine." I told Milana and stood up.

Milana stood and we walked away. I looked back at Autua, she was next to Halia on the mat, with her eyes closed.

Milana saw me, and looked back. "You are blessed."

I smiled, knowing I was.

The sun was low, yet still shining over the trees. I showed Milana the plants, and rubbed the leaves between my fingers.

"This plant also grew at the old camp." I told her.

"I know how to use it." she said, and looked at the sky. "I will go back."

"Come back and see your family." I told her.

Milana nodded. "I will." She started to speak, then stopped.

I knew what she thought. "I will travel soon." I told her.

"Good."

I put many plants into a basket, also pouches of medicines. "Take this."

Milana took the basket in her hand. "I will put these into the large basket you made for me."

I wrapped my arms around her, then let go. "Travel well."

Milana smiled, "I will come back to see Halia when I return!"

"Halia will be happy to see you!"

Later when darkness came, Autua lay our sleeping baby on her mat, and we went to sit by the fire pit. I put my arm around Autua, and she leaned her head on my chest. We listened to the fire, and the sounds around us, yet did not speak. I moved Autua to sit on my legs, and looked into her face. She was more beautiful to me now. I saw the lines around her eyes when she smiled, then leaned forward, and put my lips on her nose. She put her hands on each side of my face.

"I am happy." she told me.

"I am happy." I said, and smiled.

MANY BIG MOONS PASSED, and we watched Halia grow. She sat up, and moved on her hands and bent legs now. She spoke to us, and to the birds, yet we did not know what she said. We fed her soft fruit, and cooked fish, and Halia smacked her lips when she ate. She still drank from Autua, then slept much during the day in our hut. I watched her, and saw her teacher with her many times.

"He is a big man." I told Autua.

"Good," she said, "he will protect her as you do."

I nodded, "Yes, I will protect you and Halia."

Autua grabbed my hand, "When will Milana return?"

"Soon." I said.

"I want her to see Halia."

"I need to teach her medicine, and find new plants that grow on this island." I told her.

Autua looked at me.

"Do you want to travel with me and Milana?" I asked.

"Yes." Autua said, nodding.

"I will take you to see your mother and father." I told her.

Autua smiled, "My family will see Halia."

"Yes." I was happy Autua was pleased.

"When we return," Autua said, and squeezed my hand, "a child will join us."

"A child?"

Autua looked down at her belly, "I grow a child."

I looked down at her belly, then up to her, and she was smiling.

"I am blessed!" I yelled, and heard birds cry back.

Autua laughed, then looked at the hut, "She still sleeps."

Autua put her arms around my neck, and wrapped her legs around my waist. I carried her to the mat under the tree, where I lay her down.

"You are a good woman." I told her, and dropped my cloth to the ground.

"You are a good man." She whispered to me, as I lay down next to her.

A VILLAGER CAME to our hut for medicine, and told us that Milana had returned.

"I will see her!" I told Autua, "and tell her we will travel with her."

Autua nodded, "Go! Halia sleeps."

I put my lips on her face, then ran down the trail. As I passed by huts, I waved to the villagers, and to the old woman that helped Autua. The trail stopped at the fire pit, and old men sat by the fire sipping tea.

"Where is Kekoa?"

"He took warriors up there." a man said, and pointed to the trail that led into the mountain.

I knew he went to build huts for the villagers. I nodded, "Thank you."

I walked back up the trail, then over to the warriors' hut. Milana stood with her back to me, bending down over her large medicine basket.

"Milana!" I called.

She stood up, and turned to see me. "Kai!"

I walked to her with a big smile, "Welcome!"

"How is Halia?"

"She grows big," I said and smiled, "Autua grows another baby!"

Milana clapped me on the arm, "My family grows!"

I laughed, "I was told this baby will be a boy, and a great warrior!"

"Good!" she said, "I will train him!"

"When will you and Kekoa travel?"

"When the moon is big," she answered, "we will take the warriors around the island."

"We will travel with you." I told her.

Milana pulled her eyebrows together, "Can Autua and Halia do this?"

"Yes." I said, "we walk many places with Halia."

Milana nodded, thinking of this, "Kekoa will be happy you travel with us."

"I will prepare my family," I told her.

"Yes, prepare," Milana said, "I will send a warrior to tell you when we leave."

I looked at her basket, "It is heavy?"

"Yes."

"I will carry medicine also!" I told her.

"Good!"

"I go." I told her, and clapped her arm.

"I will send a warrior." she called out as I left.

I ran up the trail, then to the stream where I would follow it to my hut. I told Autua that we would travel soon, then looked at her belly.

"We do not have to travel now."

She shook her head, "The baby is little"

"You will not be sick?"

"I am strong."

I nodded, "You are strong, yet Halia is growing big."

"I will carry her." she said, "in my cloth."

"I will make a basket to carry her." I told her.

"A basket?" She asked.

"Many women use baskets on my old island." I said.

"The women carry babies in baskets?" she asked, "how do they work with a heavy basket in their hand?"

"The basket is on your back." I told her.

"Oh," she said, "I want to see this."

I WOVE a basket for Autua's back with holes where Halia's legs would hang down, and I held it next to Halia.

"I will weave it up to here." I said, and pointed to the baby's neck, "she can turn her head to look."

I wove the back of the basket, then large straps that went over Autua's shoulders, and held it out to look at it.

"It will scratch her skin." I thought.

I walked into the hut, where Autua filled a small basket, with dried fish and fruit.

"It will scratch her skin." I told her.

She looked at it, and put her hand inside to feel where Halia would sit, then turned and grabbed the cloth she carried Halia in. Autua put the cloth down into the basket to cover the woven basket.

"She will sit here when she is awake." she said, "and when she sleeps, I will carry her in the cloth on my chest."

I looked at Halia sitting on a mat playing, "Put her in."

I slipped the straps over my shoulders, Autua picked her up, and put her into the basket.

"Put your legs in!" Autua said to her, and showed Halia where her feet went in the holes.

I felt Halia grab my hair with both hands, then her little feet started kicking me in the back.

"She is happy!" Autua said.

Halia pulled my hair and laughed, so I took big steps bouncing her up and down. Halia squealed and kicked fast, laughing and grabbing my hair tighter.

"Take her out." I said, and stopped.

Autua reached to get her, yet Halia held tightly to my hair, and fought her mother.

"I will walk outside with her, then we will take her out, and check her skin." I said, and walked out of the hut.

"She looks over your shoulder!" Autua said.

I felt Halia lean down and put a wet mouth on my shoulder, and I put my hand back on her head. She raised her head, and looked to the side, where Autua stood.

"She sees the birds." Autua said.

"I will walk with her." I walked to see the plants in the dirt, then behind the hut, and around to the front again.

Autua followed us, and laughed, "She looks at the trees, and smiles."

I laughed, "She will travel well."

I took the basket from my back, so that we could lift Halia out. She was not happy, and started to cry.

"Come my baby." Autua said to her, and lifted her up to her chest.

I looked at Halia, and found a spot on her leg where the basket rubbed it.

"I will put more cloth here." I said.

"I will weave a mat for her head," Autua said, "the sun made her eyes small."

I PUT a ball of dried mud, covered in leaves, in my medicine basket. We would take a little each day, make it soft with water, and rub it on Halia's skin so the sun would not burn her. I strapped a bed roll, and water pouches to it, and looked inside to see it was not yet full.

"Good," I thought, "I will carry Milana's medicine also."

I felt my heart pound, and looked at Autua. She rubbed Halia's back, and sang a song as Halia went to sleep. I bit my lip and wondered if I was prepared. I looked at the basket that Halia would travel in, and saw a small round mat with strings that Autua had woven for Halia's head.

"We are prepared." I thought.

When the darkness came down, I stood outside, looking at the moon.

"It is big!" I told Autua. I had not traveled after I brought Autua to this village, and I was happy to walk around the island again.

Autua joined me, and looked up. "It is big."

"Your mother and father will be happy to see you."

She put her arm around my waist, "I will be happy also."

I put my arms around her, and leaned my head on her shoulder. She put both arms around my waist, and pulled me to her.

"Will we join when we travel?" she asked.

I thought of this, "We do not want young warriors to hear you scream!"

Autua leaned her head back and laughed, "We will join now."

CHAPTER 10

*B*efore the sun came over the mountain, a warrior had come
to our hut.

"We will leave." he said.

"Tell Kekoa we will come." I told him, and he ran back down the
trail.

Autua and I woke Halia to put her in the basket. She lay her head
on Autua's shoulder, and she went back to sleep. Autua grabbed a
small basket with food, and I put my medicine basket on with the
bedroll and water pouches. We walked out to the trail, just as the sun
started to light the trees. Now, as we reached the village, only Milana
was here. Kekoa and the warriors were walking ahead on the trail.

"Welcome!" Milana said, "are you ready to travel?"

"Yes," I answered, "where is your medicine?"

"In my basket."

"I will carry it." I told her.

"Later, we must travel to Kekoa now." Milana answered, and
headed up the trail. I let Autua walk behind Milana, then I followed.
Halia still slept, and she gently rocked, as Autua walked.

The air felt good. It was still cool from the night, yet I knew when
the sun was high, it would be hot. I wondered if Autua would tire of

carrying Halia on her back. I also wondered if the basket would rub her skin.

"I will look for marks on her shoulders and back, when we stop." I thought.

I was glad to be traveling again, and happy that Autua was with me. Milana walked next to Autua, and they talked. I heard Autua speak of her mother and father, and of showing them Halia. I heard Milana speak of her grandfather, and how Kekoa had been her father on the new island. They laughed and enjoyed the trail. I did also, and thought of sleeping on a bedroll this night, looking up at the lights in the sky.

I SAW Halia's head raise up, and look around. She traveled in the basket, looking over Autua's shoulder. I walked behind her, and rubbed my hand on her hair.

"Halia!" I said, she turned her head to me, and smiled.

We reached the big rock that blocked the trail, and I lifted Halia from the basket.

"Take your baskets off." I told them.

Milana and Autua slipped the baskets from their shoulders, and put them down.

"Go through, I will bring Halia, then the baskets."

I watched the women turn with their backs to the mountain, and squeeze through to the trail on the other side. I picked Halia up and held her over my head, she laughed, then I squeezed between the mountain and the rock.

"Your daughter!" I said, as I handed Halia to Autua.

I went back, and carried each basket over my head, to the other side. We put them on, and Halia into hers, before walking again. She was happy to look around as we traveled, we walked under trees, and many birds sang. I sang also, Halia smiled, yet we had not walked far when she began to cry.

"She is hungry." Autua said.

"We will stop." Milana told her, and walked off the trail.

I followed, and lifted Halia out of the basket.

Autua took the basket off her back, "My back is hot!"

I looked at Autua's skin, and her shoulders had marks.

"I will carry Halia now." I told her.

"No!" Milana said, "I will carry her!"

I smiled at her, "Who will carry your basket?"

Milana looked at me, "You will!"

"I will." Autua said, as she put Halia on her breast.

Milana and I sat, and watched Halia drink. Her little hands pushed at Autua's chest as she drank.

"Do you hurt?" Milana asked.

Autua laughed, "No."

I pulled medicine from Milana's basket, put it in mine, then lifted Milana's basket with one hand. "Good."

Milana drank from her water pouch, and gave it to Autua. We drank water and rested, until Halia was finished.

"We go." Milana said, and put the baby's basket on her back.

I lifted Halia up, sat her down in the basket, then she grabbed Milana's long hair and squealed.

We laughed as Milana started to walk, and Halia began kicking and making noise.

"She holds my hair tightly!" Milana cried out.

Autua looked at me, and we laughed more.

"Do you want me to carry her?" Autua asked.

"No!" Milana said, and kept walking.

We were still in the shade of the trees, and the wind blowing from the water kept us cool. I breathed in the smell of it, and thought of swimming.

"We will swim at your village." I told Autua.

"Yes." she called back.

We walked along the trail, and again I heard Milana and Autua talking.

"When Milana speaks with Autua," I thought, "she is not a warrior."

Milana talked of family and babies, not of being a warrior and battles. We walked until the sun was over our heads, and Halia began to cry again.

"We will stop." I called out.

Milana walked to a large tree and sat down. Autua walked to her, and lifted Halia from the basket.

"I am hungry." I told them.

Autua handed me Halia, and slipped the basket from her shoulders. She sat the small basket she carried in her hand on the dirt, and took dried fish and fruit out. She handed it to me and Milana.

"Eat." Autua told her.

Milana smiled, "You are a mother!"

Autua cut a piece of soft fruit for Halia. Halia took the fruit in her hand, shoved it in her mouth, moving her mouth and sucking on it. She was happy and made much noise as juice ran down her face.

"She eats well." Milana said, then rubbed juice from Halia's chin.

We enjoyed the rest and watching Halia, as we ate.

MILANA LED Autua and me up the trail, through the canyon. Halia enjoyed the ride on Milana's back, looking from side to side at the trees, birds and flowers. We reached the trail that had water running down over it. Milana stopped and looked up.

"Kekoa and the men are there." she said, "they have left many foot marks in the mud."

I looked to see where they had climbed beside the water, that made its way down the mountain.

"I will carry Haila." I told Milana.

Milana nodded, "I will climb ahead."

She squatted down, and I lifted Halia out, then Autua took the basket.

"Give me your basket." Milana said to me.

My basket carried all the medicine, and was heavy, yet I knew Milana could climb with it. I slipped it from my shoulders, and gave it to her. She put it on, and started up. I put the Halia's basket on my back, and squatted down for Autua to lift her in.

"She is in." Autua said, and I felt Halia grabbing my hair.

"You go ahead of me." I told her.

Autua started to climb, following Milana's foot steps up the mountain, and I went behind her. Autua took a step and slipped on the mud, as she started to fall forward, I grabbed her from behind and pulled her up.

"Oh!" she cried out, and grabbed my hands, "Thank you!"

Halia laughed after being bounced in her basket, and Autua looked at her.

"She enjoys this!

We started to climb again, and as I went up, Halia held tighter to my hair and squealed.

"I see them!" Milana yelled to us, then disappeared over the top.

Autua reached the top, stepped up on the flat area, then turned to give me her hand.

I took it and she pulled at me.

"Thank you." I told her. She smiled, and looked beautiful.

Her face was warm from the climb, and her eyes sparkled.

"Give me Halia." she said, and lifted her from the basket. She put Halia on her hip, and walked to where Milana, Kekoa and the warriors were. I followed, looking at my woman and daughter, and feeling blessed to have my family.

"Welcome!" Kekoa called out. He sat wet, drying himself on a rock, and watched his men bath in the pool.

I looked around, and saw many huts. "You built these?"

Kekoa smiled, "Yes! Your family will have a hut this night."

I walked to him, and clapped him on the arm, "Thank you."

Milana and Autua had already walked into the water, and Autua held Halia into it, so she could kick her feet and splash.

"Your daughter gets big!" Kekoa said, as he watched Halia play in the water.

"She enjoys traveling!" I told him, then took off the basket, and walked to the water.

"Here." Autua said to me, and held out Halia.

I took the baby in my arms, and Autua swam in the water and

splashed at Milana. I watched them kick water at each other, then go under to wash themselves. Autua swam back to me, and I handed Halia to her. I swam into the water, and put my head under. It felt good, and I came up to see Milana had joined Autua.

"I am glad they are close," I thought, "Milana needs a sister."

We sat by a small fire, and ate. Halia slept in Autua's arms, and Milana sat next to them. I sat on the other side of Autua, enjoying my family, Milana and Kekoa. I was happy to be with them. Kekoa spoke with his warriors of making spears.

"The men that watch the island." he told them, "need more spears."

"I will teach you to fight." Milana told Autua.

"Teach me to make medicine." Autua said.

"Kai will teach you medicine."

"I will have you and Kai teach me." Autua said, and smiled at her.

Milana looked at Autua, and nodded, "I will do this."

I watched Milana, she smiled at Autua and spoke softly to her. My eyes felt tired, so I put my hand on Autua's back.

"I will go to the hut."

Autua turned to me and nodded, "I am tired also."

We walked into a hut. Autua put the bed roll on the floor, and we lay down.

"I am glad we travel." Autua said, and turned to me.

Halia slept between us.

"I am glad also." I told her, and put my hand on her arm, then lifted her to lay on me.

She lifted her cloth up, and whispered, "I will not scream."

I OPENED MY EYES, it was dark inside the hut, yet I saw light outside in the sky. Kekoa's heavy steps came closer, and he walked to the doorway.

"We go to the warriors' camp." Kekoa said.

I raised up, and looked at him. "I will see you there."

He nodded, and walked away to join his men. Halia moved, and rubbed her eyes.

"Halia." I whispered, and she opened her eyes to look at me.

"Come." I said, and held out my arms.

She sat up, and I grabbed her. I put my nose in her hair, and breathed in. She smelled sweet, and her hair was warm and soft. I squeezed her, and put my lips on her forehead. Autua sat up, and Halia put her arms out.

"She wants to drink." Autua said, and took her from me.

When Halia was done, we rolled up the blanket, and left the hut. Milana stood by the fire pit, which still had hot wood in it.

"Tea?"

"Yes." We said.

We ate fruit, and gave some to Halia, then sipped at our tea. The sun's light was over the mountain now.

"We go." Milana said, and put dirt on the fire pit.

I carried Halia in her basket, following the women down the muddy mountain side, and soon we walked again on the dry trail through the canyon.

The trail stopped at a cliff above the water. We looked down to see the waves crashing on rocks below, then took the trail along the top of the cliff. The wind came strongly from the water, and blew our hair as we walked. Halia started to cry.

"She does not like the wind." I said.

"I will put her on my chest." Autua said, and stopped.

I lifted Halia out of the basket, and grabbed the cloth for Autua, who put it over her shoulder. Autua held out her arms, and I gave Halia to her. She slipped her inside the cloth and Halia's head rested against her mother's chest.

"She is happy." Autua said, and we started walking again.

I LOOKED out over the sea for the big boat, yet did not see it. I watched the waves roll in, heard them crash, and smelled the water. I saw the sea birds fly down to fish in the water, and heard other birds cry out as they flew by. I had not seen the sea much, after we built our hut next to the mountain, now I wanted to see it again.

"I want a hut by the water." I told Autua.

She stopped, and waited for me to step beside her.

"I will build a hut by the water, so we can live there also." I said.

Autua raised her eyebrows, "A hut by the mountain, and a hut by the water?"

"Yes." I said.

She smiled, "I like that!"

"I will not build it close to the village." I told her, and laughed.

The sun was over our heads, Milana walked quickly, and was far ahead now. Autua and I enjoyed walking along the trail, and speaking of the new hut we would build.

"Will you fish?" she asked.

"I will give medicine to the villagers, and they will give me fish."

"You fish in the pool by the waterfall." She said.

"I do not like to fish on boats." I told her, "my brothers will tell you this."

"I do not see Milana." Autua said.

"She will join Kekoa."

"I like her." Autua told me.

"She is not a warrior with you."

"She was with her grandfather, then Kekoa," Autua said, "she had no women to be with."

"I met Milana when she was a child," I told her, "she wanted to be a medicine woman then."

Autua smiled, "She looks at Halia with a mother's eyes."

I shook my head, "Milana will not join with a man and have children."

Autua looked at me and nodded.

"Milana a mother!" I laughed.

"She will be a good mother." Autua said.

Autua and I walked down the trail slowly, as we had done, when I took her to my village. We enjoyed talking, and looking at the island. I gathered leaves for tea, and we stopped to feed and play with Halia. I felt a blanket surround us, like the sun warming us, and I was covered in the happiness of the day. We laughed, and my heart brought water into my eyes.

Autua looked at me, stopped, and put her hand on my arm, "Are you sad?"

I smiled, and shook my head, "I am happy."

She nodded, and took my hand. We walked, and listened to our baby talk to the birds.

"Milana!" Autua pointed down to the sand.

I looked and saw Milana standing near Kekoa, and the warriors. We soon reached where the trail went down the cliff to the sand.

"Milana!" Autua yelled, Milana looked up, and ran to us.

We carefully stepped down the cliff, and when we reached Milana, she put her arms out to Halia.

"Come!" Milana said, and swung her to sit on her hip, then walked ahead of us to Kekoa.

Autua looked at me, and smiled.

I shook my head, "No!"

"WELCOME!" Kekoa said when he saw us,

I looked at the young warriors, "Have they seen boats?"

Kekoa shook his head, "They have not, and do not want to stay."

I looked at the young men, and knew they did not want to stay, yet they must protect the island.

"I will take men to build a hut on the cliff." Milana told me, and pointed up.

"We will make more spears." Kekoa said, "when we have finished, we will take the warriors that have lived here, and leave others."

I watched the young warriors' faces, and saw they were not happy to stay.

"I will speak at the fire pit this night." I told him, and he nodded.

We feasted on fish, sea plants and shells. When the night sky came, many lights shone in it, and we sat around a big fire on the sand. I felt the ancestors near, and knew I must speak to the men. I stood and raised my arms.

"Ancestors!" I yelled, "you are with us, and we ask you to guide us, and protect us."

I closed my eyes, and felt a great warrior stand beside me.

"We will watch for the boats that travel on the sea. The men will come, make villages, and live on our island." I said in a low voice.

I heard the men yell out, "No!" "We will stop them!"

Then behind my eyes I saw men, women and children laid out after they had passed.

"They will smile, yet they will bring sickness." I told them.

I opened my eyes, "I saw many villagers that had passed from sickness," I looked at the men, "elders, women and babies!"

The warriors shouted out!

I put my arms up, "We must prepare to hide our families, and protect the villages."

"We will keep the sickness out of our villages!" the men yelled.

The great warrior left me, I felt tired and sat.

Autua looked at Halia, "The sickness cannot come to this island!"

Milana put her arm around Autua's shoulders, "We will fight them!"

Kekoa stood up and looked at his men. "When a boat comes, you will run to the village, and hide the families."

His warriors stood and shouted, "We will fight!"

Kekoa yelled loudly, "You will hide the villagers, then fight!"

"Yes!" "Yes!" they answered, and began to speak of this.

Kekoa sat down, "We will prepare." he said, looked out to the sea, then to me. "We need warriors in each village."

"Yes." Milana said.

Kekoa looked at her, "We must now train chiefs."

"Chiefs?" she asked.

"I am old, and you cannot be in all the villages," he said, "we will train chiefs for this island, and also send them back to protect the old island."

Milana nodded.

"They will lead the warriors, and train more."

I thought of what the old woman told me, and nodded, "Yes, my son will be a chief."

I was quiet, and watched the others speak. My thoughts were of the holy man when he asked me to learn medicine, of when I met Kekoa and Milana, and then came to this island to meet Autua.

"The ancestors have guided me," I thought, "and now they will guide my son."

I knew he would be a warrior, that Milana and Kekoa would train him, and he would be a great chief. I knew as the ancestors had guided me, I would guide my son after I passed. I looked up at the dark sky, and saw the lights shining down.

"Are you ancestors?" I thought, "watching us?"

I looked at Autua, and Halia was asleep in her arms.

"We sleep now." I told her.

She stood, I grabbed our baskets and we walked back up the cliff. I put our bed roll down, and we lay down with Halia between us.

"Are you tired?" I asked her.

"Yes."

I rolled on my side, and put my arm across Halia and Autua. Autua closed her eyes, and I did also.

THE SKY WAS STILL DARK when I woke. I saw Kekoa, Milana and the warriors sleeping on the cliff also. I stood and saw the moon shine down on the water. It rolled across the sand where we sat around the fire pit, and crashed against the cliff below.

"Kai." I heard Autua call quietly. I walked to her, and she stood.

"I go there." she pointed into the trees.

I nodded, and sat down next to Halia. My daughter's eyes were closed, and her mouth smiled with lips like Autua's. She slept with her arms stretched out, and I wondered if she would be a medicine woman, a mother, or a warrior like Milana.

"Can I see..?" I asked my teacher. I had not finished asking, when my teacher showed me a woman with hair like Autua, and many children running around her.

"Oh!" I said.

I felt a hand on my shoulder, and Autua sat down next to me.

"Halia will have many children." I told her.

"She is blessed." Autua answered.

"I am blessed." I said, and we lay back down to sleep.

When the sun rose, the water had gone away from the cliff, and we walked down to the sand. Kekoa, Milana and the warriors sat eating.

"We will build a hut." Kekoa said, then stood.

Autua fed Halia while we ate, and we watched Kekoa and Milana climb up the cliff with the men. Kekoa cut tree branches and palm leaves for the men to carry. Milana pointed to where the hut would be built.

We finished eating, "I will help them." I told Autua, and ran up the cliff.

"I will help," I told Milana.

"Good, " she said, and smiled, "I will help Autua."

I laughed, "Go!" and pointed down.

"The wind blows strong here," Kekoa said, "we will tie the hut to the trees."

I helped weave the branches together, tie them to the trees, then tied many palm leaves to cover the top and sides. Kekoa bent over, and walked in.

"It is not big, yet the warriors will be dry." he said.

I bent over and walked in, "It is good."

I looked down on the sand, saw Halia sitting by the water, splashing her feet in it and digging in the wet sand with her hands. Autua and Milana sat next to her. Kekoa followed me, and looked down.

"Milana has a woman friend now."

I nodded, "Autua said she will join with a man."

Kekoa leaned his head back, and laughed loud, "No! Milana will not join with a man!"

Autua and Milana heard Kekoa laugh, and looked up. I waved to them, and Kekoa put his hand on my shoulder.

"Such a man must be strong!" he said, and laughed again.

I shook my head, and laughed with him.

Kekoa gathered his men, "We will make a pile of spears by the hut this day, and leave when the sun rises."

The men nodded, began to look for straight branches to make spears, and Kekoa looked at me, "We will leave the men here prepared."

I nodded, "How can I help?"

"Ask the ancestors to protect them." he said.

"I will do this," I told him, "at the fire pit so all the men will hear."

WE SAT AROUND THE FIRE, Kekoa looked at me, then stood. He looked at his men, and called out the names of some, "Come to stand with me."

The young warriors stood by him.

"You will stay and watch for the boats. Each day you will train for battle, run and swim. You must stay strong," he told them, "be ready to warn the villagers."

The men called out, "Yes!" "We will do this!"

Kekoa nodded, "When the moon is big, I will send men to stay here, and you will return to the village."

The men were pleased with this.

"I will also pick men to be chiefs," Kekoa said, "I will look for men that are ready to train warriors, and lead them to fight."

A strong young warrior shouted out, "I am ready!"

The men laughed, and Kekoa looked at the young warrior. "I will test you to see who is ready," he told them, "train well, be strong!"

The men yelled out, and were happy. Kekoa waved for me to stand. I stood and looked at his men, then put my arms up.

"Ancestors!" I called, "stay with these men, and protect them."

The men were quiet.

"Help them see the boats, and warn the villages."

Kekoa spoke loudly, "When a boat comes, send a warrior to the village through the mountain, and a warrior to the village here." he pointed down the sand.

I sat down, and Kekoa walked to his men. I saw Halia's tired eyes, and looked at Autua.

"We will sleep."

Autua nodded and stood up. Milana stood up also, and leaned over to put her lips on Halia's face.

"Sleep well." she said, as we walked toward the cliff.

We lay on our blanket, and Halia drank from Autua, then fell asleep. Autua rubbed Halia's back, and looked at me. I knew that she wanted to join with me.

"Come." I whispered to her, and pulled my cloth up.

She smiled, and moved over Halia to me. She put her hands on my hips, and lifted herself to sit on me, and I felt us join. She moved on me, I closed my eyes, and leaned my head back. She put her hands on my chest, and moved faster. I had no thoughts, I was in her and felt nothing else.

I heard her breath faster, she began to make noise, and I put my hand over her mouth as she pushed herself down hard. She pounded her body on me, I felt her shake, and my water came as she fell on my chest. My heart pounded hard, and I felt Autua's heart pounding hard also.

We lay quietly, I felt her warm body on me, and wetness on my chest. I put my hand under her cloth, and felt the water from her breast. She raised up, looked at the wet cloth over her breast, and smiled. The moon shone on her hair, and lit her face. My heart warmed, and I was happy to be with her. I pulled her to me, then slept with her in my arms.

HALIA CRIED, and we woke. Halia sat, looking at us, with water coming from her eyes. I lay on my side against Autua's back, with my arm over her. Autua pulled Halia down to her, so she could drink. I looked over Autua's shoulder, and watched Halia drink from her mother's breast. I heard Kekoa, Milana and the warriors down on the sand.

"Good." I thought, and pushed myself against Autua. I pulled her cloth up, and felt her warm skin against me. Autua made a noise, she put her hand back on my hip, and

pushed against me. We joined again, and finished quickly.

When Halia was full, she sat up happy to look around. I rolled up our bed roll, and carried our baskets down the cliff.

Autua followed me with Halia.

"Are you hungry?" Milana asked.

Autua nodded, and Milana handed us fruit.

Kekoa's men stood around him, he stood tall, with his head above his warriors. He looked at me, and yelled out. "We go."

I held my hand up to him, and he walked ahead of his warriors down the sand. Autua fed Halia fruit as she ate, and I quickly ate mine. Milana stood watching Halia eat.

"You cannot travel fast with a baby." she said.

"If the boat comes, we will travel fast." Autua told her.

"We will be ready." I said.

"Good." Milana said, and smiled at Halia, "I will protect this girl."

"Halia has a strong father." Autua said, and looked at me.

"You and Halia will be safe." I told Autua, and looked at Milana.

I knew she would care for them, if I passed in battle. Soon we walked down the sand, and Autua told Milana of her family. She named brothers that I did not know, and I was surprised to hear this.

"You did not tell me this!" I said.

"I wanted to leave the village!" Autua told me.

"I have a brother for you." Autua said, and looked at Milana.

"I do not want a man."

"He is a good man." Autua said.

"He is not joined?" Milana asked.

"He wanted a woman, yet she did not join with him."

"Did she join with another?" Milana asked.

"Yes, and his heart hurt, so my brother left and made a hut away from the village."

"Does he fish?" Milana asked.

"He built a large pool, that fills with water from the sea, and fish swim into it."

"I want to see this." I told them.

"The grandfathers do not go in boats," Autua said and looked at me, "they fish in this pool."

"I did not see him when we lived here." I said.

"You watched only me." Autua said.

I thought of this, and how quickly we left her village. "The ancestors told me to watch over you."

Autua stopped, and looked at me, "You did not tell me this."

I laughed, "I wanted to join with you!"

Milana shook her head, and laughed at us, "What have you not told me?"

WE LOOKED AHEAD, saw rocks coming down to the water, and many tall palm trees.

"My village." Autua said, and pointed to the rocks.

We climbed to the top of the rocks, and looked down on the village. Kekoa and his men stood around the fire pit with villagers.

"My father!" Autua pointed to a man at the fire pit.

"Father!" she yelled, and they looked up at us.

"Autua!" came a man's voice, and many villagers walked to us.

Autua handed me Halia, climbed quickly down, and ran to her father. Autua put her arms around him, as I climbed down the rocks with Halia and Milana.

"Welcome!" her father said, and looked at Halia in my arms. "This is Autua's child!"

He walked closer, and Halia leaned back against me. "She has Autua's hair." I told him.

"She looks like Autua." her father said.

"Mother!" I heard Autua cry, and saw her mother walking to her.

Autua ran to her, put her arms around her mother, then leaned back.

"I have a child."

Autua's mother looked around her, and saw me with Halia. "Come!"

Autua's mother smiled, and put her arms out to Halia. I stretched my arms out, to put Halia in her hands, and Halia turned her head to look at me.

"This is your grandmother." I told her.

Halia did not cry as she was held by her grandmother, yet looked at Autua, standing next to her. Autua put her arms around her mother and Halia, while her father and I watched.

"She is happy." he told me.

I looked at him, "She grows a boy in her belly."

"She grows a baby!" Her father yelled out, with a big smile

THE VILLAGE MEN FISHED, and the women prepared much food. A great fire was made in the fire pit, and there was much laughter and talk. I watched the young warriors bring smiles to the women, and knew some would join. Autua's father brought the strong fruit juice, and we began to drink.

"You are a good son." Autua's father told me, and handed me the juice.

"I am glad Autua joined with me." I told him, and leaned my head back, to take a big drink.

"What of the boats?" her father asked.

"We will speak of that when the sun rises." Kekoa answered, and took the juice from me.

I smiled at Kekoa, he knew this night was to celebrate. The women gave us hot fish from the fire, and passed palm leaves with cold fish and fruit. I saw Autua and Milana, who held Halia, with women laughing.

"This is a good night." I told Kekoa.

"A good night!" he said, and took a drink of juice.

After we ate, I stood up, and grabbed for Kekoa's shoulder.

"The juice is strong!" I said, and he laughed.

I raised my arms and spoke, "Great Father and Mother, we thank you for this village, and the fish that we eat."

The villagers stopped speaking, and listened to me.

"Ancestors we thank you for guiding and protecting us."

I looked at Autua and Milana across the fire pit.

"You are in our hearts, and we ask you to join us, so that we can speak to you."

I dropped my arms, and looked into the darkness. I saw ancestors standing next to many villagers, and I saw a man standing in the darkness, looking at Autua.

"Is this Sael's father?" I thought, then the man walked across the sand to her, and I knew he was not an ancestor.

Autua saw him, and cried out "Ehu!"

He stepped to her, and she put her arms around him. I saw her step back, show Halia to him, and also Milana. He leaned over Halia to see her face, put his hand on her hair, then looked back at Milana. Autua looked at me, and waved for me to come. I walked to her, and she grabbed my arm.

"Ehu!" she said, and he looked at me, "this is Halia's father."

He had a big smile, and his eyes sparkled. His skin was dark, and his hair was tied back, yet I saw it had waves like his sister.

"He is my brother, Ehu." Autua said, and smiled at him.

"Welcome." he said, he was tall like me, and strong.

"I did not see you when I lived here." I told him.

He smiled again, looked at Autua, then back at me. "I saw you as you watched over my sister."

I nodded.

"Thank you." he told me and looked back at Autua. "I am not in the village much."

"He built his hut away from the village." Autua told Milana.

I knew she wanted Milana to know this was the brother that had not joined with the woman he wanted.

"Autua told us you have a large pool with fish." I said.

"Yes."

"I would like to see this."

"I will take you!" he said, and smiled at Milana.

Milana smiled, and looked down.

"We will go when the sun rises." Autua told him, "Go and drink juice with the men!"

She pushed my arm at her brother, and I looked at her. She waved her hand for us to leave.

"Come," Ehu told me, "the women will talk of us now!" and he laughed.

As we walked away, I heard Autua and Milana laugh, with the other women.

CHAPTER 11

⚮

*E*hu and I walked to the fire pit.

"This is Ehu." I told Kekoa.

"Welcome!" Kekoa said, and looked at him.

"I am Autua's brother," Ehu said, "I do not live in the village."

I told Kekoa of Ehu's pool with fish.

"I want to see this." Kekoa said.

"I will take you when the sun rises." Ehu said, then looked at me, "Is Milana joined with a man?"

Kekoa laughed.

Ehu looked at Kekoa, then back to me.

"No, she is a warrior." I told him.

Ehu raised his eyebrows, "A woman warrior!"

"She trains warriors!" Kekoa told him, "she will throw you on the sand, and put a blade to your throat!"

"She is a small woman!" Ehu said.

I laughed, "I have seen her do this!"

He shook his head, and looked at Milana. He did not speak more of her, yet I saw him watch her. I looked at Milana, and saw her again, as the woman I had wanted to join with.

"She is beautiful." I thought, yet was glad that she had not joined with me.

The sun rose, and I stood at the fire pit with Kekoa and Ehu.

"Are the women ready?" Kekoa asked me.

"Yes." I said, and pointed to them walking toward us.

"Good!" Ehu said, and watched them.

When Autua reached us, she held open Halia's mouth, "Look."

I looked in Halia's mouth where Autua's finger pointed, and saw a small tooth under the skin.

"She grows a tooth!" I said.

"She rubbed her finger on it, and cried." Autua told me. I looked at Halia, and she chewed on her finger.

"We go." Ehu said, and grabbed Milana's hand.

Milana pulled her hand away, looking at him with an angry face.

"I will lead you!" Ehu told her.

"I walk with Autua!" Milana said, and stepped back.

Kekoa put his elbow in my side, and looked at me. His eyes laughed, yet he was quiet.

"We go!" Autua said, holding Halia on her hip, and started to walk.

Milana walked next to Autua, and Ehu quickly walked on Autua's other side. Kekoa and I stood looking at them. Kekoa shook his head, and I laughed quietly.

"She will not join with a man!" Kekoa said.

THE SKY HAD MANY CLOUDS, and the air was cool. I smelled the sea, and listened to the loud birds cry as they flew. Kekoa and I walked behind Autua, Milana and Ehu.

"I will train the villagers to hide in the mountain, and we will build more huts there." he told me.

"You will build more huts?"

"Yes." he said, "they will need more, and my warriors will make spears to fight."

I listened to him speak, telling me of preparing the villagers to travel and hide. My heart was sad that our islands could not enjoy peace.

"There is peace now." my teacher whispered.

"Yes," I thought, "there is peace now."

We walked by the water where the sand went up high from it, and I looked up, yet could not see over it. Ehu led Autua and Milana up to large rocks at the top of the sand, and we followed. I stood at the top, and saw large rocks on both sides of a small stream, that led away from the waves to a large pool of water. The pool of water also had large rocks around it, and an old man sat on one, with a string in the water. The old man waved, and Ehu waved back.

"I dug this." Ehu pointed to the stream, "and dug the pool."

"It is large." Kekoa told him.

Ehu nodded, "It is good I am strong!" He said and looked at Milana.

Autua walked to the pool, "There are fish!"

"How do the fish come to the pool?" I asked.

Ehu looked at me and smiled.

"When the waves come here", he pointed to the sand where we stood, "the waves push water into the pool, and fish swim into it."

"When the waves leave, the fish cannot swim out!" Kekoa shouted, and clapped Ehu on the arm.

"I have also fished, and put fish in the pool to live," Ehu said, "now there are many fish."

I saw a hut behind the pool, "Your hut?"

Ehu nodded, "Yes."

We walked around the pool, and looked at many fish swimming in it. Some small, and some big.

"This is good for the grandfathers." I said.

"They enjoy fishing here." he told me.

Autua walked to Ehu's hut, and pointed to a spear hanging on it. "Father's spear!"

Autua looked at the spear, and reached out to touch the rope wrapped around it.

"It is old." she said.

"Our grandfather used it for big fish." Ehu said.

Kekoa walked to it, and lifted it from the hut. "This is strong wood from the mountain."

Ehu nodded.

Kekoa felt the tip, and looked at him, "This is a good spear for battle."

"I am not a warrior," Ehu said, and looked at Milana.

Kekoa hung the spear back, and walked to Ehu. "I will speak to you, and the villagers."

Ehu looked at him, "Will we fight?"

"When men come with the big boat," Kekoa answered, "we must protect the villagers."

Kekoa put his hand on Ehu's shoulder, "You are strong, and must be a chief in your village."

Ehu pulled his eyebrows together.

"Come." Kekoa said, and started walking back to the village.

Ehu looked at me.

"He will speak of this in the village." I told him, then looked at Autua, "We go."

Ehu and I followed Autua and Milana back to the village. Ehu was quiet, and I listened to Autua and Milana talk of Halia growing teeth.

"Now Ehu has no peace!" I thought.

KEKOA AND MILANA trained warriors on the sand, I sat with Autua, Halia and Ehu watching them.

"She is a warrior." Ehu said.

"Yes." I agreed, watching Milana throw a man to the sand.

"I am not a warrior," he told me, "I cannot be a chief!"

Autua looked at me, "How can Ehu be a chief?"

"Kekoa did not tell me this," I said, and looked at Ehu, "he is a great warrior, so I know he picks well."

Ehu shook his head, "I am surprised he picked me."

Autua put her hand on his shoulder, "You are a good man, and strong. Kekoa saw this."

. . .

WHEN FLAMES ROSE UP out of the fire pit, Kekoa stood and spoke to the villagers."My warriors will be here, yet you need a chief." Kekoa told them.

"What will the chief do?" a man asked.

"When you hide in the mountain, the chief will stay with the warriors. He will bring you fresh fish, tell you of battles, and when it is safe to leave the mountain. He will be your eyes."

"We can fish!" a man cried out.

"You will not fish on boats when the big boat is here." Kekoa said.

"Oh." and the man was quiet.

"Who will be our chief?" A young warrior asked.

Kekoa looked at him, "I will tell you after I have watched you more," then he looked at Ehu, "For the villagers, Ehu will be chief!"

The villagers looked at Ehu, were quiet, then one shouted, "He will be a good chief!"

"Will you do this?" Kekoa asked Ehu.

Ehu stood straight, and pulled his shoulders back, "I will do this."

Many village men shouted out, and stepped forward to clap him on the arm. Then Kekoa raised an arm, and the men were quiet.

"My warriors will watch the island and fight," he said looking at them, then back at the villagers, "you will watch the mountain trail, and fight the men that travel where you are."

The men shouted out, "We will!"

I looked around at the men, now speaking of battle, then looked at the grandmothers, women and children standing behind them. I saw Autua talking to her mother, and I walked to her.

"We will fight?" Autua asked me.

"When the boat brings men, we will fight."

Autua's mother grabbed her arm, and I saw her hand shake.

"There is peace now," I told her, "do not think of this."

"We are prepared." Autua said, and put her hand over her mothers.

Her mother nodded, "I may pass before this boat comes!"

Autua laughed, "I may pass before the boat comes!"

They both smiled now, and Halia leaned her head on Autua's shoulder.

"We will sleep." I told her.

WHEN THE SUN ROSE, Kekoa took the warriors, and many village men to the mountain. Milana trained young men on the sand, and I left Autua with her mother, to walk through the village and give medicine. Many villagers wanted tea to help them sleep, and some said their head hurt.

"They cannot be happy now." I thought, "they think of battles, and hiding in the mountain."

"The strong will live," my teacher said, "and the villagers that pass will guide them."

I was glad that my mother and father guided me now, "Thank you." I told them.

MANY SUNS PASSED, and Autua spent the days with her family. I sat on the sand, and looked at the waves.

"I will swim!" I thought, "with Autua!"

I found Autua outside her mother's hut.

"Can you swim?" I asked.

"Halia sleeps." her mother said, "go."

Autua walked to me, and we went down the trail to the water. I took her hand and we ran in, diving under a wave, and came up behind it.

"The water is warm!" she said, and lay back with her arms and legs out.

I lay back also, and went up and down with the water. A wave came to us, and we swam under it.

"I want to go back." Autua said, after she came up.

I looked at her, "I want to sleep in our hut." she told me.

I pulled her to me, and she wrapped her legs around my waist. "You want to sleep?"

Autua laughed, "Sleep," and, "join with you!"

I put my lips on her forehead, "We will go."

I told Kekoa and Milana that I would take Autua back to our village.

"She grows a child." Milana said, "she will rest there."

"We will not go," Kekoa said, "I will train Ehu to be a chief," and he looked at Milana, "Milana will train the young villagers to be warriors."

AUTUA PUT her arms around her mother, then her father, and Milana. Milana leaned in to put her lips on Halia, and Halia grabbed her long hair.

"She will not leave!" Milana said, and laughed.

Ehu stepped to me, and clapped my arm. "Travel well brother."

I smiled, "We will return after our son comes."

"Yes." Autua said, and grabbed my hand.

We walked down the trail beside the sea, and did not speak, only Halia talked to the birds. We climbed up the cliff, and traveled along it, before turning into the mountain. Halia now slept, and I picked more leaves for tea, then saw a small fruit tree.

"Do you want this?" I asked Autua.

She looked at it, then nodded. "We will need fruit for our children, yet if we hide in the mountain..." she stopped, and water came into her eyes.

I stepped to her, and pulled her to my chest, "Do not think of this."

She nodded, and looked into my eyes.

"I will protect you and our children." I told her.

She felt small in my arms, and I looked over her shoulder at Halia sleeping in the basket.

"I will protect my family." I told her again.

Autua leaned her head on my chest, "I am glad you are strong."

I dug into the dirt carefully, to take the tree from it. Autua rubbed her finger on a leaf.

"It will grow many fruit." she said.

We traveled under the trees through the mountain, and the wind from the sea did not find us. My body was hot, and wet with water. I looked back at Autua, her face was also wet, and I saw Halia moving to sit up again.

"We will stop." I told her.

I rolled out the blanket, and Autua sat down. I lifted Halia from the basket, and sat her down on the blanket. She looked around, then at her mother and started to cry. Autua sat Halia on her legs, and leaned her back to rest on her arm, then let her drink.

I pulled dried fish from the small basket Autua carried, and saw that fresh fruit was in the basket also.

"My mother gave us fruit for Halia." Autua told me.

"Good." I said, and handed Autua a strip of dried fish to eat.

I ate my fish and watched Halia drink.

"Are you well?" I asked Autua.

She smiled at me, "I am well, yet I am tired."

I gave her my water pouch, "Drink."

I looked around, and saw a flat area away from the trail.

"We will sleep there." I pointed.

"I can travel." she told me.

I shook my head, "We will rest and enjoy this day. I will make a small fire, and we will sleep when the sun does."

"Thank you." she said, and smiled.

After Halia ate her fruit and played, I moved the blanket back to the flat area, and gathered wood for the fire. Autua lay down with Halia, and soon slept. After I finished putting the wood in a pile, I leaned against a tree by them.

I closed my eyes, and listened. I heard birds shake the leaves in trees as they landed on the branches, then heard their feathers as they flew away. I heard them call out to each other, some were happy sounds, and some were protecting their nests with angry calls. I heard the stream of water down in the canyon. I breathed in the air, and smelled sweet blossoms, then took off my sandals to feel the cool dirt.

"Bring your self back to this, when you think of fighting." my teacher whispered.

I took in a slow big breath, and blew it out.

"We are guiding you." she said, "we are with you."

I felt a soft peace fall on me, and soon heard no more.

I AWOKE to see Autua feeding Halia at her breast again.

"She is hungry!" Autua said, "She grows fast."

"I will gather plants to eat." I said, and stood up.

I walked down the hill, to the stream and looked.

"There!" I saw the small plant that grows by the water. I pulled many leaves from the plants, yet left the roots down in the wet mud. I looked at the water and saw small fish, then a large fish swam under a plant in the stream. I quickly reached down to grab the fish. I caught it, held tight, then threw it on the dirt.

"I will feed my family this night!"

I returned to Autua. "Look!" I showed her the fish and she was happy.

When the fish was cooked, Autua blew on it, and put it in Halia's mouth. She moved her mouth, chewing and swallowing, then put her hand out for more.

"Good," I told Autua.

We watched the small fire, and I was happy that Autua and Halia had fresh fish this night. I put my arm around Autua and Halia, and called out to the ancestors,

"Thank you for the fish! Protect us and guide us to our hut when the sun rises."

Autua smiled, and Halia looked with big eyes, across the fire.

I looked across the fire, and saw an ancestor. He was a strong warrior, and bright like the moon.

"I protect Halia." he told me without speaking.

"Thank you." I said, and he went back into the darkness.

"Halia saw the ancestor that will protect her," I told Autua, "he is a warrior!"

.   .   .

WE TRAVELED, stopped for Halia to eat and rest, and when the sun was behind the water, we came to the village. We quickly walked by the stream up to our hut, and Autua took Halia in.

"Do you want a fire?" I asked her.

"No."

We were tired. Autua took Halia from the basket, and we went to the pool by the rock, to wash.

"She will sleep well." Autua told me, as she put Halia into the cool water.

Halia hit her hands on the water, splashed, and laughed. Autua and I washed, and we walked back to the hut. Autua let Halia drink, then she slept, and Autua lay her down.

"Are you hungry?"

"No." I said, and we lay on our bed to sleep.

AUTUA WOKE ME, "Your son wants fish." she told me.

I rubbed my eyes, and looked at her. She lay on her side, looking at me, and Halia drank from her breast.

"We will go to the village and get fish." she said.

I nodded.

She smiled, "I grow Halia, and our son."

I looked at our daughter drinking from her breast, and then Autua moved her to the other breast. I shook my head, and wondered how women grew babies.

"I will get many fish for you." I told her.

I walked from the hut, and saw the small tree branches heavy with fruit. I dug the dirt, put the new fruit tree in, then put water on the roots.

"We have much fruit." Autua said, holding Halia on her hip.

"I will take fruit to the villagers." I told her.

"I will dry it also." she said.

I picked fruit and handed them to Autua, then she put them in the sun under a mat.

"I hide them from the birds." she told me.

I gathered more fruit for the basket Autua carried in her hand, lifted Halia into the basket on Autua's back, and put my medicine basket on.

"Ready?"

THE MOON GREW LARGE, then small, and was large again when Kekoa and Milana returned to our village. Milana walked to our hut, and brought fish.

"Thank you." Autua said, and took them.

"Your belly has grown!" Milana said.

"The baby moves." Autua put Milana's hand on it.

"Oh!" Milana cried out, "he is strong!"

"He will be a chief," I told her, "and you will train him to be a warrior."

Milana looked at me, and did not smile, "I will train him to be a fierce warrior."

She heard Halia, and looked at her.

"She stands!"

Halia held a branch at the doorway, stepped toward her, then sat down.

Milana squatted down to pick her up, and stood, "She is heavy!"

Autua and I laughed.

"Yes," Autua said, "soon I will not carry her."

I rubbed Autua's back, "You carry our son, I will carry Halia."

We sat on a blanket under the tree, and Milana told us of Kekoa training Ehu to be chief.

"He taught him to use your grandfather's spear." she said, "he is strong, and threw it well."

"I do not want to speak of fighting." Autua said.

Milana reached over, and put her hand on Autua's shoulder, "We will speak of your plants!" and pointed to the fruit trees, and many other plants in the dirt by our hut.

"They are happy!" Milana said.

I laughed, "Yes they are!"

We walked to them, and I picked fruit to put in Milana's basket.

"I have leaves for tea in the hut." I said, and ran into the hut.

I gathered the dry leaves from a basket, put them in a pouch, then walked out and stopped. I saw Milana put her arm around Autua, and hold Halia in her other. Autua lay her head on Milana's shoulder. I ran to her.

"Are you well?"

Autua raised her head, "I am tired."

Milana looked at me, "Take her to the village," she said, "the women will care for Halia, and Autua will rest."

"I will care for Halia." I said.

Autua shook her head, "We will live in the village now."

I looked carefully at her, and saw darkness under her eyes. "You look tired."

"Your boy grows big, and I do not sleep well."

I nodded, "I will build a hut there."

"Good!" Milana said.

"Do you want the hut by the water?" I asked.

She nodded, "Yes," she smiled, "I will watch you swim."

"I will get warriors, and we will build the hut with you." Milana told me.

I looked into Autua's eyes, "Do you need medicine?"

"No," she said, and reached out her hand to me, "I need rest."

I HELD Halia and we stood by our hut, watching Milana walk back to the village. I turned to Autua, and she looked at me.

"Speak to me when you are tired," I told her, "I will help."

"You help me much," she said, "yet mothers and grandmothers, talk to me of what you cannot."

"Oh," I said, and pulled her to me, " I did not think of this."

When darkness fell and Halia slept, I gave Autua much fish and plants to eat. We sat by the fire pit, and I rubbed her back with my hand.

"Our son is strong," I said, when I saw her belly move.

"I am strong also." she said, and looked at me, "I am not tired now."

I pulled her to me, "Will you join with me?"

She looked at me and smiled. I picked her up, and carried her to the mat under the tree.

"I will sit on you." she said.

I pulled off my cloth, and lay down on my back. She stood beside me, I watched her pull her cloth over her head, and saw her large breasts and belly. She put her foot over the side of me, and sat down. Her skin felt hot on me, and I moved into her.

She laughed, "You are ready!"

I put my hands on her hips, sat up to put my lips on hers, and looked at her. "You are beautiful."

She smiled, put her hands on my chest, and pushed me down.

I laughed, and felt her move on me as we joined. After, she lay on her side next to me, and looked at me.

"I will scream in the village." She said.

I laughed, "The villagers will know we are happy!"

AUTUA, Halia and I walked to the village when the sun rose. Milana joined us at the fire pit. Fishing boats were pulled out of the water, and I looked past them, to the other side of the village.

"We will build there." I pointed to palm trees, that grew on sand high above the water.

"I will have the men gather branches, and palm leaves." Milana told me.

"It is near the village, yet no other huts are close." I told Autua.

"I am happy." she said and smiled.

Autua and Halia sat and watched, as Milana and the men wove branches together. I tied them to the trees, then we covered the hut with palm leaves, and put rocks around the bottom. Many villagers watched, and when the hut was finished, they brought mats for the inside. The men pulled a large log over, to sit in front of it.

"Thank you!" I told them.

Autua carried Halia to the log, and stood her next to it. Halia grabbed the log and walked along it, then sat on the dirt, and looked at the villagers. Women came with children to play with Halia, and gave Autua fruit and fish from their baskets. I looked at Milana and the men.

"We are glad to live in the village." I told them.

THE VILLAGE WOMEN and grandmothers watched Halia with the other children. When Halia started to walk, they clapped their hands and were happy. Men gave us fish when they came in from the sea, and I spoke at the fire pit, asking the ancestors to bless us. When Milana trained warriors on the sand, I ran with them, then swam in the waves.

"You are strong." Autua said, when she saw me walk to her.

She rubbed her hand on my belly, "it is hard." she said, "mine is also."

I felt her belly, the skin was tight and hard with child.

"Do you have pain?"

"When I walk it hurts here." she said, and pointed down.

"I will carry you."

She laughed, "No! I will walk and stay strong."

MANY DAYS PASSED, and we enjoyed living in the village. I had run with the warriors this day before they left for the mountain, then swam, and now sat watching Autua and Halia on the sand.

Halia ran to me, her little legs moved quickly. I looked past her to Autua, she walked slowly with her legs apart, and she put her hand on her back. Her belly was large and hung low.

"Are you in pain?" I asked when I saw her face.

She nodded, "Your son is ready to join us."

I grabbed her arm and Halia's hand, and we walked slowly, into the village.

"Your son comes?" a man called, and I smiled.

Many villagers watched us walk to the old woman's hut, then

Autua stopped. She leaned down and put her lips on Halia, stood up slowly, and I felt her fingers dig into my arm. She looked into my eyes, and I saw pain. Pua, a village woman that had watched Halia, grabbed her hand and asked her to play with her children, then took her away.

"Thank you." Autua said with a quiet voice, then she leaned her head on my chest.

"I will give you a son." she whispered.

I did not want her to feel this pain, yet I knew she must.

She looked up at me, "I am strong."

I leaned down and put my lips on hers, then we heard the old woman call out.

"Are you ready?" the old woman asked.

Autua turned to her, and nodded. I grabbed her arm, and walked with her to the old woman.

"Bring strong tea." the old woman told me, and walked with Autua into the hut

I brought tea to the old woman, and looked in to see Autua standing with women around her. The old woman took the tea and waved me away, so I walked across to a hut, and sat down with villagers. I was glad that Halia played with children, and was watched by their mother.

I sat and listened to the villagers speak of women bringing babies in. The sun traveled lower to the water, and I wondered how Autua was. Milana and Kekoa returned from the mountain, and walked to me.

"She brings in the baby?" Milana asked.

I nodded, and Kekoa clapped me hard on the back. "She will give us a strong boy to train!"

I heard her scream, and jumped up.

"Sit!" an old man told me, and I sat down.

Milana sat next to me, and I looked at her, "You will not help her?"

Milana shook her head, "I cannot help with this."

Autua started to scream again, and Kekoa shook his head.

"I do not like to hear women scream," Kekoa said, "I go to my hut."

Milana looked at me, "I will wait."

We sat and listened. It was quiet, then I heard Autua make noise, and begin to scream again. I stood up and walked close to the hut, and when she stopped screaming, I heard her breathing hard. I looked in the hut, and saw Autua squatting with a woman on each side, holding her arms. Autua looked up at me, then her face filled with pain and she closed her eyes, the old woman looked at me, and yelled, "Go!"

I turned to walk back to Milana, and I heard Autua scream loud and long. My legs started to shake, my ears did not hear, and as I looked at Milana, blackness came upon me.

"Wake!" I heard, then felt water pour on my face. I opened my eyes and looked up. Milana grabbed my hand and pulled me up. I had dirt on my back, and I shook my head to wake up.

She pulled me to a log, "Sit!"

A woman handed me water to drink.

"Do not watch a woman when she brings a child." I heard a man say, and the villagers laughed.

I sat next to Milana, and sipped water. "Halia came in faster, it was not as hard on Autua." I told her.

Milana looked at me, "She is strong, she will not leave us."

My heard pounded, I looked back at the hut.

"Ancestors protect her, and my son." I said.

As night came, I heard Autua scream again and again. I stood and walked away from Milana. My heart still pounded in my chest, and I could not eat or drink.

"Mother!" I called in my thoughts, "protect Autua."

I looked at the old woman's hut, and saw my mother's face in the darkness. I knew she watched over Autua.

"Thank you." I told her.

Autua screamed again, and now when she finished, I heard the women in the hut yell out,

"He is here!" "Your son is with us!"

I ran back to Milana, and she stood with me as we listened. Autua made no sound, yet a baby's cry could be heard. My eyes filled with water, I wanted to hear Autua call for me. Milana grabbed my arm, we looked at the hut, and waited. I wanted to see Autua, and know she was good. Then I heard her voice, it was small, yet my heart was happy.

"See your son!" she called to me.

Milana laughed, and I saw water in her eyes. We walked to the old woman's hut, and the villagers followed. I looked in and saw Autua laying on a mat, while the women washed our son, then handed him to her. She looked at him, rubbed his face, and smiled.

"He looks like Kai." she said, and looked up at me, with a big smile.

Milana and I sat down on each side of Autua, and looked at the baby.

"He is big!" Milana said.

Autua nodded, "He was hard to bring in!"

"That is why you screamed more than with Halia?" I asked.

Autua smiled at me, and nodded. "He is big like his father."

I looked at her, and water came into my eyes. "I am glad you are strong."

I rubbed her arm, and looked at our baby. He was big, with dark hair and eyes like me, and now searched for his mother's breast.

"Here." Autua said, and gently turned his head to find her breast.

"He drinks!" Milana said.

We laughed, and watched him. My heart was happy, I was blessed with another child.

"Thank you." I thought again, and again, "Thank you."

I watched Autua and our son until they slept.

"I will sleep here." Milana whispered to me.

I left to find Halia sleeping, with Pua's children on a mat.

"I will watch her," she said, "when Autua is ready, I will bring Halia to her."

"Thank you." I told her, and walked to my hut.

I LOOKED into the night sky, saw many lights shining, and the moon was big. The water gently rolled on to the sand, and brought a soft wind, to blow across the village. I enjoyed my walk, then reached the hut. It was dark, and quiet. No sounds came from Halia, or Autua. I thought of when I traveled around the island by myself, living as a medicine man. I was happy then, yet now that Autua was my woman, and I was a father, my heart had grown and I was glad to have my new life.

"I am happy to grow old with Autua," I thought, "and watch our children get big."

CHAPTER 12

I awoke to sounds of men, pushing their boats into the
water, and I walked out of my hut to see them. They
waved, and called out.

"We get fish for the feast!"

I waved and nodded. It was a good day, the sky was clear.

"What name will my son have?" I thought, and walked quickly back
to the old woman's hut, saw many women outside talking, and
looking in to see the new baby.

"You are blessed with a son!" a woman told me, as I walked
through them, to see Autua.

I stood in the doorway, and the old woman called out, "Come".

Autua lay on her side, with our boy drinking from her breast. She
looked at me, and smiled.

"He is good."

I squatted down and looked at him, he had much dark hair, and his
skin was dark.

I put my hand on his head, and he pulled away from his mother.

"He knows you." Autua said.

"What name have you given him?" I asked.

"Ikaika"

"Ikaika" I said, "I like this."

I looked around, "Where is Milana?"

"She left to join Kekoa."

"I am glad she stayed with you." I told her.

"She is my sister." she said, and smiled.

I sat with Autua until she and Ikaika slept, then I walked out. Many villagers clapped me on the arms, and talked of the feast this night. I went to the fire pit to join the men, ate fish, and sipped tea.

"Kai!" I heard Kekoa yell.

I stood to see him walking quickly to me, Milana and the warriors followed.

"You have a son!" he called.

I smiled and nodded.

He reached me now, and clapped me on the arm.

"A son!" he yelled, and his warriors yelled out also.

Kekoa looked at me, "His name?"

"His name is Ikaika."

"Yes!" he yelled again, "He will be a strong chief!"

I nodded, "He is big!"

Kekoa laughed loud, "Milana told me of this! We will feast this night, and ask the ancestors to watch over him!"

Kekoa sat down, "I am hungry!"

A grandfather passed him fish, and we watched him eat. Kekoa stood tall to look over mens' heads, with large, strong arms and legs. The many marks on his body from battle wounds, and the dark marks drawn on his skin, made him look fierce. He was a warrior that no man could fight, and win.

"You will train my son to be a warrior." I told him.

He nodded his head as he ate.

"I will teach him to make medicine as a child, then you will take him."

Kekoa nodded, "I will make him a great warrior and chief."

. . .

TALL FLAMES ROSE out of the fire pit, and lights from the fire flew into the air. All the villagers had gathered, and children ran around us on the sand. Pua held Halia on her hip, and she laughed at the children playing with her. I stood with Kekoa, and waited for Autua to bring our son.

"She comes!" a villager said.

I looked, and saw Milana and the old woman, walk on each side of Autua. Autua held our baby, and walked slowly to us. She smiled at me, and I was glad to see her. The villagers let her pass, and she stopped in front of me.

She raised our son up to me and said, "I give you a son!"

The villagers yelled out, as I took him into my hands. I looked at him, and he looked back, yet was quiet.

I held him up so that the villagers could see, "His name is Ikaika!"

Then I handed him back to Autua, and raised my hands again.

"Great Father and Mother," I called, "Thank you for all you give us."

The villagers called out also, "Thank you!"

"Ancestors protect my son, guide him, and make him a strong chief for our village."

Kekoa's warriors called out, and the villagers yelled also. The warriors began to dance, and Kekoa passed me a gourd with strong juice in it.

"Drink!" he told me, and I raised the gourd up, leaned my head back and poured it in.

I laughed when the juice ran out of my mouth. Kekoa clapped me on the back, and I looked at Autua. Her eyes were happy, and she nodded.

"I will take Ikaika to our hut." she said.

Milana looked at me, "I will watch over her."

I nodded and leaned down, to see our son in Autua's arms.

"Thank you." I told her.

She leaned to me, and put her lips on my face, "Thank you."

Milana took Halia from Pua, then walked with Autua, and the baby to our hut. I was happy this night, I drank more juice, and talked much with Kekoa.

. . .

MANY BIG MOONS PASSED, and we did not return to our hut by the mountain. Autua and I were happy to live by the water, and with the villagers, that now were our family. I learned their names, and gave them medicines for their sickness and pains. Autua had much help with Halia and Ikaika. Pua watched Halia with her children, and brought us fruit. The men gave us fish after they brought their boats up on the sand. Autua sat on the log in front of our hut, watched me swim, and we watched Milana train the warriors.

Kekoa's family also lived in this village, and we now knew his children and his woman. He had many grandchildren, and I laughed, when I heard them call out, "Grandfather!"

Our son grew large and soft, Halia liked him much, and he smiled at her.

"I will gather fruit and plants from the mountain." I told Autua. I had not walked to our old hut since Ikaika came.

"I will come." she said, and put the baby in a cloth on her chest to carry.

Halia held my hand as we walked through the village, then she saw Pua's children, and pulled her hand away. I held her shoulders, and she wiggled to run away. Pua waved for her to come, and I let Halia run to them.

"We go to our old hut." I told her.

"Go." she said, and I watched Halia happy to join her children.

WE WALKED BESIDE THE STREAM, and then saw the big rock. Water poured through the rocks I piled below it, and as we passed them, we saw much water around the big rock.

"It is big." I said.

We saw our hut sitting up on the hill. The fruit trees stood as high as the hut now, and the plants were large, some had grown down the hill.

"There is much fruit!" Autua said.

139

We filled our baskets with fruit and plants, then sat under the tree in the shade.

Autua let Ikaika drink, then he slept in her arms. I reached over, and pushed her hair behind her ear.

"I am happy." I told her.

She smiled, and lay Ikaika down on the cloth to sleep. She moved to sit by me, and took my hand.

"I am happy." she said, and put my hand on her breast.

I pulled her to me, "We made our children here."

"Give me a child now." she whispered in my ear, and lay on her back.

I looked at my beautiful woman.

"I will think of this." I thought, "when I am old."

I joined with her, and put my hand on her mouth, when she began to scream.

We washed in the pool of water, and stood looking down at Ikaika sleeping.

"We will come back to gather more fruit." I told her.

"And make children." she said, and took my hand.

Autua picked up Ikaika, and we walked back to the village. We returned to Pua's hut, she pointed inside, where we saw Halia and the children sleeping.

"When they wake, I will bring her." Pua said.

"Thank you." Autua told her.

We walked down the trail, and saw Milana and Kekoa at the warrior hut making spears with the men, and we waved to them.

As we got closer to the water, I saw dark clouds over the sea.

"Look," I told Autua, "strong winds will blow this night."

HALIA AND IKAIKA GREW, and Autua was again big with child. Halia played with the village girls, and I saw that her heart followed her own mother's. Halia wanted babies, I knew she would be the woman I saw with Autua's hair, and many children running around her. Ikaika watched for Milana to bring men to train on the sand, then ran to her. She played with him on the sand, and she showed him how to move his body for protection during a fight, and how to roll when he fell.

"Good!" I yelled, and clapped for him.

Milana smiled big, and was glad he learned quickly.

Kekoa's bones started to hurt, and I gave his woman tea to make.

"I am a warrior, yet when Ikaika is a man, I will protect the villagers in the mountains." he said, "I will not walk to a battle with these old legs!"

As I had learned much from the holy man and Konani, I also learned much from Kekoa. He was a warrior, yet he was a good man that cared for his family. He told me that his oldest son was training to be a warrior, and had passed when he fell on his own spear. The sons that followed did not want to be warriors, they fished for the village now. His daughters had joined, and given him many grand-children.

"When I pass," he told me, "I will be ready to guide my family."

I looked at him, and heard my teacher speak, then I told him.

"You protect and guide this village, and you will train many more warriors before you pass."

He smiled, "I will not soon pass?"

I shook my head, "Your body will be old..." I stopped, and saw him blocking the trail with his own body between the rock and the mountain.

"You will pass as you protect the villagers."

He did not smile now, he looked at me and nodded.

"I would pass to protect my family."

"And many villagers." I told him.

This pleased Kekoa, and he nodded again.

"I am glad to know this."

AUTUA GAVE ME A GIRL, and she named her Luana. She was a beautiful baby with Autua's skin, and my dark hair. She had a quiet cry when she came to us, looked at her mother and father, then was happy to lay at her mother's breast. As she grew, she watched and listened, and learned to talk and walk before Halia or Ikaika had.

I watched Luana follow Autua in the hut, and saw Autua touch a fruit to feel if it was soft, then Luana reached her small hand to touch it. Then Autua picked a leaf from a basket and smelled it. Luana waited, watching her mother, then Autua put the leaf under her nose and Luana smelled it as her mother had.

"She will be a medicine woman." my teacher said.

I looked at Luana and knew she would.

"Yes," I thought, "I will teach her."

Each night I helped Autua lay the children down for sleep. I spoke to the ancestors.

"Protect them while they sleep."

Then Autua sang to them, and we rubbed their backs. They slept well, and we were thankful for our family.

"MILANA!" I screamed. I sat up on my mat, not yet awake.

Autua lay on the mat, looking at me. I did not know what I had seen in my sleep, yet I wanted to warn Milana. I stood up.

"I will see Milana." I said. I leaned down to put my lips on Autua,

"Sleep." I told her, and stepped over our children sleeping on their mats. I quietly walked to the doorway and looked back, Autua's eyes were closed again.

I walked out, and felt the cool wind blow to me from the water. The sky was yet dark with many lights shining. I looked up and saw the moon, with small clouds flying near it, and I took in a big breath. My heart pounded,

"Milana" I said quietly, and walked down the sand to the warrior's hut.

I heard loud sounds of men sleeping, walked to the doorway, and looked to see Milana. She was not there, and I stepped back.

"Where is she?" I thought. Then I heard steps and turned. She walked from the village toward me.

"What is this?" she asked.

"Are you well?" I asked her.

She stopped with her hands on her hips, and pulled her eyebrows together.

"I am well."

I looked at her, "You do not sleep?"

She smiled, "I talked to Noa."

I looked at her, wondering of this.

"She will be a warrior," she said, "she wants me to train her."

I looked at her, wondering if I had seen Noa.

"Why are you not in your hut?" she asked.

"I awoke yelling your name."

Milana shook her head, "I am good."

I looked into her eyes, "I awoke, and felt you had passed."

She bit her lip, looked at me, and nodded, "I will be careful."

WHEN THE SUN ROSE, I walked to the fire pit, where Milana spoke to Kekoa of Noa.

"You think she will be a good warrior?" he asked.

Milana nodded, "Yes."

"Are there other women that want to be trained?"

"I do not know." she told him.

Kekoa did not speak, he looked out to the sea, nodding his head.

"You will build a women's hut." he said, "and tell the villagers you will also train young women that want to learn."

Milana smiled, "I will do this."

Milana, Noa, and the warriors built a women's hut, Milana and Noa now slept there, and Noa trained each day with the young men.

"Do other young women want to train?" I asked Kekoa.

He laughed, "They are making babies!"

I looked around to see many new babies, and women looking ready to bring in more children.

"The village grows." I said.

"My warriors have joined with women here," Kekoa said, "they are having families."

"This is good." I told him.

"WE NEED TO GATHER FRUIT," Autua told me, "the children will play in the village."

I looked at her, and she smiled. She liked to join with me at our hut under the trees.

"I would like that." I said.

We walked Halia, Ikaika and Luana to Pua's hut. Pua watched our children, and Autua also watched Pua's. Our children were happy to play, and ran from us. I took Autua's hand, and we walked toward the stream.

"A branch has fallen on the hut!" she cried out.

I saw a branch, heavy with fruit, had broken and fell on the hut. I walked closer to see.

"It has not broken the hut." I said, and pulled the branch down.

I looked at the many fruit on the ground,

"We must pick the fruit, and give it to the villagers."

Autua went into the hut, came out with baskets, and handed a big basket to me. We picked all the fruit from the trees, filled the baskets, then sat them by the hut.

"I will wash." she said, and walked to the pool of water. I followed her, and watched her pull the cloth, over her head. I dropped my cloth, and we stepped into the cool water. It felt good, and I put my head under. I came up, and Autua moved to me. I looked at her face, leaning forward to put my lips on it.

"You have given me beautiful children." I whispered.

I sat on a rock under the water, pulled her on me, and she wrapped her legs around my waist. She moved her hips over mine, and I pulled her down to join with me.

"You are a good man." she said, and moved with me.

The water made waves, that went away from us, and splashed on the big rock.

Autua laughed, "I am glad we have this pool."

I did not speak, I wanted only her body now. I grabbed her long hair that fell down her back, and pulled at it. She leaned back, closed her eyes, then moved hard on me. I closed my eyes, pushed back hard, and felt her body get tight. She grabbed my hair now, looking into my eyes, and screamed loudly.

Autua finished screaming, and started to laugh.

"I am glad we can join here!" She said, "I can scream and not wake the children!"

I laughed, and wrapped my arms around her. "I am glad also."

She washed our cloths, and hung them on a branch, to dry in the sun. We lay down under the trees, and I looked at her body. Her breasts were still large from feeding Luana, there were lines on her belly from growing babies, and she had beauty of the Great Mother. I moved close to rub my hand on her body, and I thought of when I wanted Milana, she did not have a soft body such as this. Autua's body felt good to me, and to our children, when she put her arms around them to hold them.

"Your body is good." I told her.

Autua smiled, "My body has made me happy."

I thought of this, "A woman's body can join with a man, and grow children."

She nodded, "I am glad to be a woman."

I put my finger in her mouth, she bit it and laughed. I rolled her over, and jumped to sit on her, holding up her arms.

"Make a baby." she called out, and I lay down, to join with her again.

"My woman wants many babies." I whispered in her ear.

"Yes!" she whispered back.

WE MADE A BABY THAT DAY, and soon Autua's belly grew big. Luana liked to put her hand on her mother's belly to feel the baby, and Halia would sit with Autua also, and laugh when she saw the baby move.

"They are young mothers!" Autua told me.

I had taken Ikaika on walks with me, to gather plants for medicine, yet he did not like this. He wanted to play warrior, and fight with the village boys. He got many cuts and marks on him, yet he was happy to fight again.

"He will be a warrior, and a chief." Autua said.

We were happy with our children, and liked to sit outside the hut, and watch them play. They ran on the sand, played in the water, and swam with the other village children. Their life had peace. I was glad of this, and did not want the peace to end, yet my heart told me one day it would. As the sun got lower to the water, we sat and watched them.

"I will make this hut bigger." I told Autua.

She nodded, "Good, we need a big hut for the children, and your medicine."

"I will ask Milana and her men to help."

"You will build it fast with their help." she said.

I put my arm around her shoulders, and looked down at her big belly. "I have not dreamed of this baby."

"This baby will be a surprise!" she said, and looked at me, "thank you for my children."

"Thank you for joining with me." I smiled at her, and looked back at the children. Ikaika wrestled in the sand with a bigger boy.

"Ouch!" he called out, and the big boy stood up. Ikaika stood rubbing his arm, and Luana ran to look at it.

"Our little medicine woman!" Autua said, and smiled.

CHAPTER 13

"Wake!" Autua screamed.

I heard her scream again, "Wake!"

I opened my eyes and saw her sitting up, she put her hand in front of my face, and it was covered in dark water.

I sat up, "What is this?"

She shook her head, and looked down. I looked also, and saw dark water on the mat.

"The old woman!" she cried out.

Halia now stood next to us, with big eyes, "What is this?"

I stood up, and put my hand down to Autua. She pulled to stand up, yet as she stood on her feet, she looked at me with fear, and fell back down.

"Bring the old woman." she said, "I cannot walk."

"Stay here!" I yelled at Halia, and saw Ikaika and Luana getting up from their mats.

I ran out into the darkness, and called to my mother.

"Mother! Be with Autua!" I ran to the old woman's hut, and stopped in the doorway.

"Wake!" I yelled, "Autua needs you!"

The old woman raised her head, and looked at me.

"She needs you!" I said again, and stepped back.

I heard villagers wake, and turned to see a man standing outside his hut.

"I am ready." the old woman said, and walked from her hut.

I left her, ran back to my hut, and saw the children sitting next to Autua. The dark water that came out of Autua, had spread over the mat, and the children sat in it.

"She is here." Autua said to me.

"The baby?"

"She is here." Autua said again.

"The old woman comes." I told her.

Autua smiled, and looked over my shoulder.

I felt her now, and turned to see Sael, standing in the darkness.

"No!" I told her, "She will stay!"

Sael smiled at her mother, and Autua reached out her hand.

"No!" I cried out, and I dropped down to look at Autua.

She smiled, and I tried to say "stay," yet my throat had closed, and my heart was pushing on my chest.

"What is this?" the old woman said.

I turned to see her.

"Look!" I yelled, and pointed to the dark water.

I turned back to Autua, and she was gone. I looked to see Sael, she was gone also.

"Autua!" "Autua!" I screamed so she would hear me.

"Come back!" I yelled, yet I knew she would not.

I heard the children cry also, "Mother!" "Mother!"

The old woman pushed through the children to see Autua, and felt her chest. She leaned down with her face by Autua's nose, and looked at me.

"She has passed."

I FELT water falling from my eyes, saw the children grabbing at their mother, and putting their heads on her. They cried out, and the old woman patted their backs, and spoke softly to them. I tried to breath, yet could not. My chest could not take in air, my heart's pain was too big.

"Autua!" I said again and again.

The children cried louder, and the old woman put her arms around them. I leaned down, put my hand on her hair, and kissed her forehead. She was warm, and looked asleep, yet she was gone. My head started to go round, I put my hands down, and pushed myself to stand. My legs shook under me, and I grabbed the hut. I stood, looking down at Autua, my children, and the old woman.

"Is this a dream?"

Then I heard sounds of villagers, and looked outside, they walked to my hut.

"No!" I cried out, and tried to walk, I leaned against the doorway, and saw Milana and Noa coming to me.

"Kai!" Milana yelled. I looked at her, shook my head, and started to run.

I RAN ALONG THE WATER, yet did not feel my feet on the sand. I heard myself yelling, yet did not know what I said. I ran as fast as I could, and when I could not see from the water in my eyes, I fell on the sand pounding my fists.

"We need her!" I yelled at the great Father, "Why did you take her?"

I lay there, heard the cries of the villagers, and knew their hearts hurt also. The water did not stop pouring from my eyes, and I screamed out.

"How will my children be happy without their mother?"

I thought of Autua, "My Autua!" I screamed again and again.

I lay on the sand yelling to the Great Father, the Great Mother, to my teacher, to my mother and father. I wanted to know how she could pass so young, and leave me and our children.

My head pounded, I had much pain in my heart, yet I knew I must be strong for the children.

"I will not be happy with out you!" I told her.

"You will be happy for our children." I heard her say.

I sat up, and saw her. The moon shined down on her, as she stood by the water.

"Autua!"

"I am with you." she said and smiled, then went away into darkness.

I sat waiting for her to return, I looked across the water and down the sand, and waited while my body shook with fear that I would not see her again.

She did not return, and as the moon traveled deep into the night, the villagers got quiet and I knew they slept.

"I do not know how to live with you gone," I whispered to her, "Help me."

I AWOKE ON THE SAND, sat up and looked around.

"It was not a dream." I thought, "she is gone."

Water ran from my eyes again.

"Autua, are you with me?" I asked, yet I did not feel her.

"How can I grow these children up?"

There was much pain in my heart, it was hard to breath, and I felt a rope around my chest yet there was not. I looked at the water and stood up.

"I will swim," and started to walk.

"Kai!" I heard, yet it was not Autua so I did not look.

I walked into the water, and felt it cold. I looked up and saw clouds covering the sun.

"Kai!" I turned to see Milana running on the sand to me.

I looked back at the water, wanted to run into it, and not return. I wanted to pass and be with Autua, yet I stood with my arms hanging down.

"Kai!" Her feet splashed water, as she ran to me. I felt her arms grab me, and pull me to her.

She shook and cried out. "Autua has left us!"

I felt her pain like my own. She leaned her head on my chest and called out. "Autua!" and I felt water fall from her eyes on my chest.

I grabbed Milana's shoulders, held her back, and looked at her.

"She came to me," I said, "I, I..." my throat closed again, and I could not speak.

"She came to you?" Milana said.

I dropped my hands, walked past her to the sand and sat.

Milana followed, "She came to you!"

I looked at her, and knew she was glad I saw her. I nodded, then fell back, and put my arms over my eyes. I did not want to be in my body, I did not want to feel the pain in my heart. I lay there with water rolling down my face. Milana sat next to me, and shook my shoulder.

"You must go to your children."

WE WALKED ALONG THE SAND, and when I saw the hut, I walked far around it to the village. Halia and Luana sat with Pua, when they saw me, they ran and grabbed my legs. Water poured from Halia's eyes, and Luana asked, "Where is mother?"

"Where is Ikaika?" I asked Pua.

"With Kekoa."

I squatted down, put my arms around my daughters, and my lips on their faces.

Pua came and took their hands, "We will eat." she told them.

"No!" Halia cried out, and held me tightly. I looked into her little face, and grabbed her and Luana tightly.

"I will come back," I told them, "I will see Ikaika now."

Water fell from Halia's eyes, and Luana looked at her.

"Halia, you must care for Luana now." I told her, and took her hand to grab her sister's.

Halia looked at her sister, and nodded.

"I will come back." I told them, and put my lips on their foreheads.

Pua gently guided them, and they looked back at me, as they walked into the hut. Milana and I watched, then walked to Kekoa's hut.

"He is at the warriors' hut." Kekoa's woman told me. I looked at her and was angry. She was a grandmother, yet Autua was young with a child in her belly.

"Autua should be here!" I thought.

We found Ikaika sitting next to Kekoa, watching the warriors make spears.

Ikaika ran to me, and Kekoa stood. I looked at Kekoa, and he held great sadness in his face. I bent down and picked up my son, he put his head on my shoulder.

"Will she come back?" he asked in a small voice.

I shook my head, "No son."

"He will start his training." Kekoa told me.

I put Ikaika down to stand by me, and looked in his face.

"Are you ready to train?"

He had water in his eyes, yet held his mouth tight, and nodded.

"He is ready." I told Kekoa.

Kekoa walked to me, and put his hand on my shoulder.

"He is young, yet I will start training him to be chief."

Milana looked at Ikaika, then me, "I will train him to be a fierce warrior."

I nodded, looking at my son, still small with little arms and legs.

"I will also care for him." Milana told me.

I watched Ikaika listen to us. "His mother has passed," I said, "he will learn to care for himself, as I did when I left my mother, to learn medicine from the holy man."

"He will do this." Kekoa said.

I squatted down to look in Ikaika's eyes. "You have many here that will teach you, and guide you," I held his shoulders, "your mother also watches over you. Know this."

He looked into my eyes and nodded. His eyes were filled with water.

"He is so young," I thought, "they are all young."

"The ancestors guide them." My teacher said.

I knew this, yet I was their father, and did not want them to suffer.

"I will not leave them," I thought, "I will help them grow."

As I thought this, I felt Autua, and knew she would be with me to guide them.

"Thank you," I whispered, and knew she heard.

THE VILLAGE HAD a feast and great fire for Autua. I did not want to go, yet I sat with my arms around my children. The villagers told my children of their mother, and asked Autua to watch over them. Many women yelled out to her, and much water came from their eyes. Then Kekoa walked to Ikaika with a branch, and handed it to him.

"Make the fire burn bright," he told him, "for your mother to see."

Ikaika stood, threw the branch in, and we watched it feed the flames. Kekoa put his hand on Ikaika's shoulder, and squeezed. I looked at my daughters, and they were tired. I stood and picked up Luana, and grabbed Halia's hand.

"They are tired." I told Kekoa.

He nodded, and looked at Milana.

Milana stood, "I will take Ikaika to my hut."

I looked at Ikaika, "Do you want to sleep there?'

He looked at Milana, then back, "Yes."

Milana and Ikaika walked away, and I told him, "Sleep well."

I took my daughters to Pua's hut, and she smiled when we entered.

"Come." she told them.

I watched them go to a mat, and lie down. Pua covered them with a blanket, and I walked out. My children were well cared for.

"Thank you." I thought.

I went to lay on the sand. I looked up at the lights in the sky, and listened to the waves. Water rolled out of my eyes, and down my face. I thought of sitting with Autua, watching the children play, and of joining with her at our mountain hut. I thought of my family sleeping side by side, now Ikaika was with Milana, my girls with Pua, and I lay by myself on the sand.

"It changed so quickly."

.   .   .

WHEN THE SUN ROSE, Kekoa's warriors carried Autua's body, to the place where the ancestors rested. Milana walked with me, and the children. We reached the side of the mountain that looked over the sea. There were piles of rocks and flowers that grew over them. Villagers began to make a place for Autua, and I did not want to see this. I did not want to think of her under rocks.

"Milana, I will take the children from this." I told her.

"Go with your father." she said.

I led them away, into the trees, so we could think of Autua here. I showed them a bird fly into it's nest, and we listened to the sounds of the baby birds. We found flowers, that smelled sweet.

"Your mother liked sweet smelling flowers." I told them.

"She put them in the hut!" Halia said.

"Yes." I smiled at her.

I heard the villagers sing for Autua, and wondered if the children should be there, yet they were happy to walk with me. We looked for pretty rocks, and I showed them plants I used for medicine. I watched them, and thought of Autua.

"We made beautiful children." I told her.

CHAPTER 14

*M*any big moons passed, my daughters stayed with Pua, and she grew them with her own children. Ikaika stayed with Milana and Noa in the warrior hut for women, and I did not return to the hut where Autua passed.

The villagers burned the mats with Autua's dark water, made new mats, and I gave the hut to a young family. I went to our mountain hut to pick fruit, yet did not stay there. I slept in my bedroll on the sand, to be near my children. I watched Halia and other girls play with babies woven from palm leaves, took Luana on walks to learn of plants, and saw Milana train Ikaika with the other warriors. The children were well cared for, and after many big moons, I knew I must tell Autua's family of her passing.

"I will travel to the other villages." I told my children. "They need medicine."

"You will return?" Halia asked.

I nodded, and smiled at them. "I will come back, and bring you surprises."

Halia and Luana clapped, "Good!"

"Bring me a spear." Ikaika told me.

I looked at him, and did not want him to pass as Kekoa's son had.

"When Milana wants you to have a spear," I said, "she will teach you to make it."

Ikaika stomped his foot, and looked angry.

"Does a warrior do this?" I asked him, his face changed, and he looked down.

I LEFT THE VILLAGE, and walked the trail around the island. I came to the young warriors that watched for the big boat, and saw they looked well. Then I walked to Autua's old village.

Ehu stood at the fire pit, and when he saw me, smiled big. "Brother!"

I looked at him, took in a big breath and blew it out. "I have to tell you..."

I stopped, bit my lip, and looked into his eyes, "Autua has passed."

"What?" Ehu shook his head, "How is this?"

I told him of her passing, and watched his face fill with pain.

"I will speak to my mother and father." He told me.

I nodded, and watched him leave. I had little medicine to give the villagers, and emptied my basket quickly. I walked to Autua's family hut, and saw many villagers standing outside. I heard cries from Autua's mother, and looked in to see her father holding her. He saw me, and shook his head. Ehu walked out.

"Tell them they are welcome to see their grandchildren." I said.

"I will."

"I leave to gather plants for medicine."

"You will not speak at the fire pit?" Ehu asked.

"My heart is not healed," I told him, "I cannot stay."

Ehu nodded, "Go brother, we will heal our hearts, then come see the children."

"I would like that," I said, and clapped his arm.

I left, and walked on the trail to the new huts by the waterfall.

"I will sleep there." I thought.

.   .   .

I BATHED IN THE POOL, and made a small fire. I was away from the sounds of a village, away from speaking with them of Autua. I wanted to be with my children, yet when I saw them, my heart hurt knowing their mother had passed. I tried to let my mind rest. I did not want to think of Autua, yet thoughts of her came each day when I awoke, and stayed with me until I lay down to sleep.

I spread out my bedroll, lay down, and closed my eyes. I wanted to feel Autua next to me. I wanted to smell her hair, and touch her soft body.

"The body that grew my children." I told the night sky.

My head hurt, and my body was tired. I did not feel this when I slept, and closed my eyes to fall into darkness.

I AWOKE and heard birds singing. I lay there, and looked at the leaves in the trees. They moved with the wind, the sun shone on them, and through them.

I sat up, and looked at the water falling into the pool.

"I will stay to watch our children grow," I told her, "yet I will be glad to pass."

A bird with twigs in its mouth flew to a branch, then put them in a nest.

"I will be happy to see you." I said.

I RETURNED TO THE VILLAGE, and gave Halia and Luana strings of small shells, to hang around their necks.

"Thank you." Halia said, then Luana smiled, "Thank you."

I smiled at them, "You are beautiful, like your mother."

Ikaika waited, and I pulled a gourd and sticks, out of my basket.

"This is for you."

He sat down, put the gourd on his legs, and pounded it with the sticks.

"You have grown!" I told him, as I watched.

He looked to see boys playing, then up to me.

157

"Go play." I told him.

"Thank you Father." He ran to the boys, showing them his new gourd.

I looked at my daughters, they were happy to stay with me.

"Your grandmother will come to see you," I told them, "make her a string of shells to wear."

Halia clapped her hands, and Luana jumped up and down. I took their hands, and we walked by the water.

"Look what I found!" the girls told me, and showed me small shells.

"Good." I told them.

They gathered shells, gave them to me, and walked ahead. I watched them, and was glad to see them smile. I saw Ikaika running with village boys, and knew my children were doing well. I stayed with my girls this day, we dug holes in the sand, and played in the water. Later, when Pua took them to eat, I sat with Milana at the fire pit.

"Autua has given me a son." Milana told me.

"He is young," I said, "he needs a mother."

I had watched Milana with Ikaika, and when she trained him, she was a warrior. She was strong and hard. Yet when training was finished, she chased him to make him laugh, and rubbed his hair with her hand.

Noa also watched over Ikaika, and cared for him as a mother. I knew the ancestors guided Autua to live in the village. After she passed, her children were well cared for by the villagers that raised them as their own.

Each night the children joined me at the fire pit, then left to sleep in their huts. I stayed by the fire, speaking with Kekoa, then he left along with the villagers. I sat by myself, watching the fire, and looking out over the waves.

The sky was dark with many lights, and I saw them move. I did not know if my eyes made them move, or if they traveled in the sky. I wondered if the ancestors traveled on the lights, or if the lights were ancestors that watched over us.

"Your daughter is with Autua," my teacher said.

"My daughter!" I jumped from the log where I sat, I was ready to run to my daughters, when my teacher said,

"Autua grew a girl baby when she passed."

I sat down again.

"You will see her when you pass." she told me.

"I would like that."

"Why did you not tell me Autua would pass?" I asked her.

"We told you," she said, "when you slept."

I shook my head, "I do not know this dream."

"You woke with fear, and called to Milana."

"I thought Milana would pass," I said, "yet it was Autua?"

"The pain for Autua's passing was great," my teacher said, "you gave the pain Milana's name, so you could wake."

I nodded, took in a breath and blew it out. "The pain was great."

"When you sleep, and the ancestors tell you family will pass," she said, "many times you wake, with a name that is not the one that will pass."

"I am glad I did not know." I told her.

WHEN THE MOON WAS BIG, Milana gathered warriors to watch for the boats.

"I must leave," she told me, and looked at Ikaika, "he cannot travel with me yet."

"I will care for him." I told her.

"Sleep in my hut with him." she told me.

Ikaika stood by me, and we watched Milana, Noa and the men get ready to leave.

"I want to go." he said.

"You will travel," I told him, "after you are big."

"Big!" Kekoa said, and put his hand on Ikaika's head.

Ikaika shook his head, and ran around Kekoa, "I will be big as Kekoa!" he told me.

Kekoa laughed, "Your father is big also."

Ikaika stopped, and looked at me, "My father is big!"

I laughed, and stepped forward to grab him, yet he jumped away.

"You are fast!" I told him.

He smiled, and ran to play with village boys.

"Your children are good." Kekoa said, "you should join with a woman."

I looked at him, "No!"

Kekoa did not smile, "You are young, you need a woman."

"I have a woman," I said, "she will welcome me when I pass."

He grabbed my arm, "Join with a woman, and be happy."

I shook my head.

"Think on this." Kekoa told me.

I ENJOYED IKAIKA. We swam in the waves, and ate at the fire pit when the sun fell. I rolled out my blanket in Milana's hut, and looked to see him. His eyes were closed, and he slept.

"How fast he sleeps!" I thought.

When the sun woke him, he grabbed fruit and ran out. He played with many boys, and they did what Ikaika told them.

"They know him as chief." my teacher said.

I watched Ikaika run with the boys after him, then stop and speak to them.

"He teaches them." I said, and watched him grab a boy, and roll on the sand. The boys laughed, yet I knew Ikaika taught them, as Milana has shown him. I did not want him to fight in battles as a chief, I did not want him to pass.

"The ancestors will protect him." My teacher told me.

"I will enjoy him now." I thought.

.   .   .

I STOOD WITH IKAIKA, and my daughters, watching the fire. We had eaten, and Pua was ready to take them to sleep in her hut.

"Will you sleep in Milana's hut with Ikaika?" Halia asked.

"Yes," I told her, "I will stay there when she and Noa travel."

"Can we sleep in your hut?" Luana asked.

I looked at my girls, then at Pua.

"Take them." she told me.

They jumped up and clapped.

Kekoa laughed loud, "You have a new family hut!"

We went to the hut, the girls moved their mats to each side of me, and Ikaika lay on his mat across from me. We had not slept in the same hut since Autua passed, and we were happy to be there.

"I want to stay with you." Halia said, and looked at me.

"I want to stay with you," I told her, "yet Pua has much to teach you."

"You can teach me," Halia said.

I reached my arms out, and pulled the girls to me. "I cannot teach you to be a woman," I told them, "you will learn to be a mother from Pua."

"Milana teaches me to be a warrior." Ikaika said, and raised up to look at me.

I looked at him, "Yes, she is a good teacher."

Luana's eyes were closed, and her breathing grew soft.

"Sleep now." I told Halia and Ikaika.

We stayed in Milana's hut. Each day we awoke, ate fruit, then the children left to play with the village boys and girls. Each night after eating, we went back to Milana's hut, and were happy to lay on our mats talking before sleep came.

"The children heal my heart." I thought as I fell asleep.

MANY SUNS HAD PASSED, when Milana, Noa and the warriors returned in the night.

"What is this?" she asked, when she and Noa walked into the hut.

I sat up, and looked at my children sleeping.

"We have enjoyed your hut." I said, and smiled.

She nodded, and threw her bed roll down.

"My tired body will enjoy it also!"

The sun rose and Ikaika woke.

"Milana!" he called out, and jumped from his mat to sit by her.

He shook her shoulder, "Milana!"

He was happy to see that she returned while he slept.

"Go!" Milana told him, and rolled away from him.

"She is tired." I told him.

Ikaika grabbed a fruit from the basket, and suddenly threw the fruit at her! The fruit hit her bed roll, yet she did not move.

"Ikaika!" I yelled, and he ran out.

Halia and Luana were now awake, and came to me.

I stood, grabbed their hands, and we walked quietly out of the hut.

"Where is Ikaika?" I asked them.

We looked for him, and saw him with the boys on the sand, then the girls went to eat fruit with Pua and her children. I sat with Kekoa at the fire pit, and told him of what Ikaika had done.

"Anger can make him a great warrior," Kekoa said, "he must learn to use it in battle, not in the village."

I nodded, and looked at Kekoa, wondering what I could do for Ikaika.

"We will teach him this." he told me.

MILANA ASKED me to sleep in her hut. I was glad to do this, and be near Ikaika. Now when she left to travel with Noa, I was there, and my girls joined us. We began to speak of Autua. They were young when she passed, and wanted to know more of her. We sat on our mats, and I spoke of her, and their sister Sael.

"What did she look like?" Halia asked.

"She was pretty like you." I said.

I told them of Autua's family in the village on the other side of the island.

"I will take you there," I said, "when you are bigger."

I spoke of my family on the old island, and how I left to learn medicine from the holy man. They wanted to know much, and each night I told them of Autua, myself, and our families. They learned the names of their families, learned of their villages, and learned of the old island. Their thoughts grew outside of this small village we were in, and I began to teach them how the ancestors guide us.

"Mother guides us." Luana said.

"She watches over you." I told her.

"I see her,"

I looked at her, and knew she saw the ancestors as I had when I was a boy.

"Good." I nodded.

MANY BIG MOONS PASSED, and the villagers were prepared by Kekoa. Milana had trained warriors, and made camps to watch the island. I spoke to the villagers at the fire pit, and told them of the boats that would come, and of the sickness.

"We will fish, grow our children, and be in peace," I said, "yet when they come, we will be ready."

I sat much with Kekoa by the fire pit now. We watched our children grow into men and women, we watched the village grow with many huts and fishing boats, and the new warriors' hut was now big and long.

AS HALIA GREW into a young woman, I looked at her and saw Autua. Halia's hair fell in waves, and had streaks of sunlight like her mothers. Her eyes turned up at the sides, and when she smiled, my heart was happy to see the smile of Autua. Many young men wanted to sit with her at the fire pit, yet she only sat with a grandson of Kekoa.

I sat with Kekoa and watched Halia and his grandson across the fire pit.

"Will they join?" Kekoa asked.

"She is young." I told him.

Kekoa laughed, "My daughter was young, yet she joined, and gave me many grandchildren!"

"Halia will have many children also," I looked at him, "I have seen this."

My old friend slapped me on the arm, and let his head fall back to laugh loudly.

"When I met the young boy that was the holy man's new assistant," he looked at me and laughed again, "I did not know you would be the father of my grandson's woman!"

I laughed loudly also, "We have traveled far together since that day!"

Kekoa and I laughed more, then spoke of many things we had done and seen. We were as older and younger brother now. I looked at him as my family, and I was his.

IKAIKA GREW BIG AND STRONG, he stood tall like me, and had dark hair and eyes. He had the dark marks of a warrior on his body, and Milana had trained him to be fierce in battle. Ikaika trained young warriors now, and Milana was well pleased with him.

He traveled with her and Noa around the island, and stayed in the camps that watched for the big boat. Milana spoke to me many times, of Autua blessing her with a son. Noa also looked on Ikaika as a son, and had taught him much. When he returned to camp after traveling, Ikaika sat with me at the fire pit.

"The men on the boat," he asked, "how do they fight?"

"They have large blades, such as Kekoa has."

Ikaika nodded, "I have seen this."

"They bring sickness that also kills."

"Tell me of this."

I told him of the sickness that made his grandfather, and Milana's grandfather pass.

Ikaika shook his head, "I cannot fight sickness."

I nodded, "Yes, and good men will carry sickness also."

"Good men?" he asked.

"Good men will also come on boats," I said.

"I will fight them."

"Protect the villagers," I told him, "hide them in the mountain."

Ikaika nodded, "I will do this," he looked at me, "I will protect them."

"Good." I told him.

LUANA HAD young men that wanted to sit with her at the fire pit, yet she sat with me.

"I want to learn medicine," she told me, "I am not ready to join and be a mother."

"Do you want to be a medicine woman?" I asked, and carefully watched her face.

She smiled, "I have seen that I will give villagers medicine."

"I have seen this also." I said and nodded, "I will teach you."

This made her happy, and her eyes were bright.

"You will be my assistant." I told her, "as I was the assistant to the holy man."

I traveled with Luanna around the island, taught her the plants, and how to make medicine. We enjoyed walking the trails as Autua and I had. Luana learned quickly, and I was pleased with how she gave medicines to the villagers.

"She will be the new medicine woman on this island," I thought, "when I am old."

"Give her the ceremony." my teacher whispered.

"The ceremony? I had not thought of this."

"Find a place on this island," my teacher said, "bring her into the circle of medicine men and women."

"I will do this." I told my teacher, and knew I must find a place on this island, where all the new medicine men and women would be given the ceremony.

I found such a place hidden high on the mountain, where a stream came down into a small pool of water. I brought Luana there, and gave her the ceremony as the holy man had done for me. She saw her teacher's face in the water, and heard her voice. Her teacher was also a woman, and after this, I watched Luana grow into a medicine woman welcomed by all the villagers.

"She will be called a holy woman." My teacher said.

I knew this would be so, and told Luana that when I am old, she will take an assistant to teach.

She smiled, "My teacher has told me this."

"IKAIKA MUST LEARN MORE OF BATTLE," Kekoa told me, "then I will make him chief."

"He has much to learn from you." I told him.

"Has Ikaika found a woman to join with?" Kekoa asked.

"He has many women that bring him fish and fruit," I said, "yet he has not met the woman he will join with."

"Will he find her on another island?" Kekoa laughed, "and never want another woman after she has passed?"

He spoke of Autua, and that I never wanted a woman after her.

"If he meets a woman such as Autua, he will not want another!" I told him.

"It is good that Ikaika trains the warriors." Kekoa said, "and travels with the men."

I nodded, "Milana is happy to stay in the village now."

Milana and Noa still lived in the hut built for women warriors. They had been joined by young women that trained, and lived with them, yet they did not travel with the men around the island.

"She teaches the women to guide the villagers to the hiding place, and protect them there." Kekoa said.

"We are well protected." I told Kekoa.

HALIA JOINED with the grandson of Kekoa, their joining was a great celebration, and Autua's family traveled from the other side of island.

Halia had a boy, then another, and now grew a baby in her belly. Luana helped Halia bring in the babies. Luana was a medicine woman, and learned to bring babies in from the old woman that helped Autua.

After Luana was trained, the old woman passed, yet Luana said the old woman still guided her. Luana had not met the man she would join with.

"I have seen his face." She said.

"I saw your mother's face also." I told her, "You will join and be a mother."

"I know this," She said. "when I am ready."

I smiled, and knew the ancestors would guide this young man to her.

KEKOA WAS GROWING OLD, I gave him medicine for his bones, yet he still stood tall and strong. He guided the villagers as a chief would, and I spoke at the fire pit as the holy man had. We had found peace in our village, and we wanted to enjoy this, knowing that a battle could come on a boat with the waves.

After Kekoa and the villagers went to their huts to sleep, I liked to sit by the fire pit. I enjoyed watching the fire grow small, then live in the hot wood at the bottom. I listened to the waves crashing on the sand, and the water coming in closer for the night. The moon was small, and the lights shone bright.

I thought of the holy man, my mother and father, and my family that lived in the flatlands on the island I left. I thought of Konani, and wondered how his family grew, and if he looked an old man now.

And my Autua, she was in my heart and thoughts each day. I felt her much, and knew she was glad that I watched over our children. My heart was healed, yet I wanted to be with her again.

I WALKED down the sand to a small hut I had built by the water. I liked to sit by it at night, speak to Autua, and tell her of our children

"I am pleased with our children." I told her, "they have grown, they have found their paths, and they are happy."

I looked up at the lights in the dark night sky, and saw a light move slowly, then stop. The light grew brighter and brighter, and my heart warmed. The light seemed to speak to me.

"Autua?"

I jumped to my feet, and looked at this light that was brighter than the others.

Water filled my eyes, and my heart was full of happiness.

"Do you come for me?" I asked Autua.

The light did not move, I watched it and felt it watched me.

"Autua?" I asked again.

The light began to move, then quickly went away into darkness. I looked hard, and did not see where it went.

"Thank you." I whispered, feeling she was with me.

I took in a big breath, and smelled the sea. I dug my feet into the sand, and felt it smooth between my toes. I looked across the dark water where it joined the sky, and felt the soft wind blow on my face.

My heart was happy, I knew Autua waited on me. I sat down, lay back on the sand, and closed my eyes. I took a slow big breath, and blew it out. My body lay quiet, and I slowly took another breath, feeling the air fill me with peace.

I felt light, as if I lifted from my body, yet I still felt all that was around me. I felt joined with the sky and the soft wind, I felt joined with the sand and the water, and I felt joined with all those that slept in the village. My heart was full.

"I am this." I told myself.

"Yes," My teacher whispered, "we all are this."

ABOUT THE AUTHOR

APRIL AUTRY

April writes about her spiritual journey, including many of her past lives.

April is an Intuitive mentor, Quantum healer, Reiki master, Yoga teacher, and teaches alignment of your Mind-Body-Soul through consciousness expansion and spiritual practices. Books, blog, shop, and services can be found on her website:

https://GalacticGrandmother.com

April enjoys reading your book reviews, so please feel free to email her at:

https://info@galacticgrandmother.com